MW01038729

SURVIVING

TO

THRIVING

The 10 Laws of Grateful Leadership

STEVE FORAN

Bulk purchase discounts, customized copies and signed copies are available by contacting the author through his website at https://www.gratitudeatwork.ca/.

ISBN 978-0-9950905-4-5

This book was published with the support of Happful.com

This book is dedicated to my mom. I love you.

CONTENTS

INTRODUCTION

THIS BOOK WAS WRITTEN for you. The words and stories contained are personal and are intended to empower you and those you lead. It consists of a set of very simple, yet powerful principles rooted in the virtue of gratitude that, when followed, will continually orient you toward thriving leadership.

Which begs the question, "Do you want to spend more time thriving and less time surviving?" It might be a no-brainer of a question, but we live at a time of unprecedented opportunity, and yet far too many people are stuck in an endless struggle of survival, trying to escape from daily living rooted in scarcity and never having enough.

For this reason alone, we need more thriving leaders now than at any time in human history. It doesn't matter if you're the CEO of Coca-Cola, or you're starting your first part-time job, or you're coaching your kids' soccer team; you are a leader. Leadership has been the source of influence and change throughout human history and has had immense impact on change, both good and bad. Whether it was the tragedy of persecution or the joy of liberation, leadership was at the core. To bring about a just, loving, compassionate world in which you and everyone else thrives, we need thriving leadership. Your thriving leadership is needed. I need your thriving leadership. Your mother, neighbour and colleague need your thriving leadership. The kid down the street and the CEO of Coca-Cola both need your thriving leadership. Quite frankly, if we are going to solve the biggest challenges our world faces, we are going to need more than just you. We need a movement of thriving leaders.

As you uncover each of The 10 Laws of Grateful Leadership, I hope you will discover that these 10 laws are life principles that will guide you and help you grow as a leader so that you can have the impact that arises from the depths of your soul.

Gratitude has been a monumental force in my life. Over the past 15 years the growing body of research around gratitude is compelling. Gratitude is a foundational leadership character trait and, according to the research, is the best predictor of thriving leadership. This is no small claim. Gratitude has transformed the lives of countless individuals, and now is the time for you and I to collectively harness the power of gratitude to solve some of the biggest challenges in our world.

I am not so naive to believe that gratitude and gratitude alone will solve all of our problems, but I'm not sure how we can solve any significant problem without it. We need more gratitude in our world, not because people are broken or need to be fixed, but because we need to thrive as a species and part of how we're wired keeps us in survival mode. Survival mode can become your reality in the blink of an eye: a child is injured in a senseless vehicle accident, your spouse gets laid off, your company falls short on projections, your doctor gives you bad news, or your babysitter calls in sick. It's at times like these that we need gratitude the most. Gratitude enables us to see the good in our life circumstances so that we can thrive and deal with the crap that is part of everyday life. Survival mode worked well when humanity lived amongst wild animals, but as we embark on sending humans to inhabit other planets, this and major world problems will only be solved if the vast majority of the population is thriving.

In this book, we've distilled how to use gratitude to build and maintain a thriving mindset. The ideas and frameworks discussed are simple. Kindergarten simple. Don't let the simplicity deceive you. There is much more we need to learn about gratitude and the mechanisms by which it works because we don't fully understand all of the intricacies. However, we don't need to wait to learn everything about gratitude and how it works in order to help people spend more time thriving and less time surviving. According to Dr. Robert Emmons, the world's leading scientific authority on gratitude, the upside is that there's no downside to being grateful.

In this book, you will not find an overwhelming regime of time consuming activities that are necessary to spend more time thriving. Instead, you'll discover a simple set of four actionable, basic habits that will take you four to eight minutes per day if you take up the challenge to embrace them. I hope the ideas in this book will challenge you to think differently about how you show up as the thriving leader you are meant to be.

While The 10 Laws of Grateful Leadership are inter-related, each chapter stands on its own and each law carries one or more implications for you. I share those implications with you and provide you with some questions for further reflection and growth.

I wrote this book for one reason. It's to help realize my dream, and my dream is simple: To inspire one billion happier people. We're not talking about the hedonistic feeling that ebbs and flows based on one's circumstances. No. We're talking about stable happiness that comes from deep-rooted joy, pervasive throughout one's life. And as you'll discover as the chapters unfold, gratitude is the key to a happier thriving life. So if you want to be a thriving _____ (you fill in the blank—mother, father, supervisor, sister, wife, coach, partner), join me, and many others, as we each build a more grateful frame of mind.

CHAPTER 1

GRATITUDE GIVES
RESPONSIBILITY A TIME-OUT

I HAD NEVER GIVEN much thought to what it would take to be a thriving leader and to live a thriving life. I wanted success. I wanted to be happy. Like many, I thought, "Work hard, get an education and take responsibility for your actions, and success will follow." This was my mantra, and it continues to be the unconscious default formula for success in the world today. Tragically, this thinking is flawed, as evidenced by the overwhelming number of people who hate what they do for work. Far too many people feel like they are trapped in an unending struggle of survival and not having enough of what they truly want in life.

While I firmly believe we live in a world where hope and happiness are justified, if you look at barometers for human happiness like the UN's World Happiness report or Gallup's results on employee engagement, that is not the picture they report.

So something is wrong. Something is fundamentally broken. Yes, we must work hard. Yes, we must take responsibility for our actions. Yes, we must get an education. The fundamental problem is that true happiness requires more, and that "more" is gratitude. We all know and understand what gratitude is, but lost from focus is its relevance and critical importance in living a happy, thriving life. Sound simple? It is. But it's not as easy as you may think. Through this book and my journey, I hope that you are able to discover how gratitude can help you spend more time thriving and less time surviving. My wish for you: true happiness.

Here's how it happened for me...

I was the oldest of five kids. Our house seemed like a three-ring circus at times because something was always going on. Mom and Dad encouraged us to bring our friends over to the house, and we had lots of relatives who would drop in, so there was never a dull moment. As the oldest, I developed a strong sense of responsibility as I grew up, and today responsibility is one of my core values. I truly believe we must hold ourselves responsible for our lives and the circumstances in which we find ourselves. While this belief is still firmly within me, fortunately I don't hold to it with absolutely certainty anymore.

Let me explain.

In days past, my sense of responsibility was accompanied by a heavy dose of judgment. I was very judgmental. For example, when I came across someone who was down on their luck and was panhandling on the street, I was at the front of the line judging them. If they asked for money, I would not give them any of my money (figuring they'd only spend it on liquor) and I'd think to myself, "This is my money! You want money, why don't you go out and get a job and earn it like I did?" I was anything but empathetic.

I had always held to the belief that if it is going to be, it is up to me. I worked very hard to earn my degree in Electrical

Engineering and for that matter everything I'd ever earned in my life. It started in grade eight when I bought my first 10-speed bike with money I saved from my paper route, and it continued throughout college as the engineering program was extremely challenging. And when I graduated, I felt I deserved it, after all the work I put in and all the sacrifices I'd made along the way. As for the engineering degree, I did recognize my wife and family for their support and encouragement, but for the most part, from my perspective, it was my degree. I did the work, therefore I deserved it.

And then my perspective changed about 15 years ago, but this change did not happen suddenly. It was gradual. Over the period of a few months I came to the realization that it was as if my life had been handed to me on a silver platter. This was an ah-ha moment for me. What is significant about this realization is that it was not brought on by a major tragedy in my life, I didn't experience nor witness extreme poverty in the developing world, I didn't experience a major health setback, nor death in my family. Nope. For me it was the simple realization that I didn't do it on my own. And after many years of thinking it was all because of me, this was a profound realization.

Years later, I hear it reflected in different ways by others. One of my favourite clients (who am I kidding, all of my clients are my favourite clients), Paul, describes his realization after our work together this way: "I used to think I had hit a home run, and then I realized I was born on third base." Paul's analogy captured how I felt, too.

The gratitude from my ah-ha moment caused a time-out for my value of responsibility. Time-out—like the time-outs we gave our kids. They were never harsh punishments (I remember the wooden spoon); instead time-outs were a natural consequence of behaviour where the child gets time to step back and think about things. For me, gratitude made me step back and reassess my value of responsibility.

Not long after my ah-ha moment, a few thought patterns became crystal clear to me that would have previously been keeping me in survival mode. These new thought patterns below further supported the overwhelming sense of joy and peace that grew out of my newfound gratitude:

MY POSSESSIONS DO NOT DEFINE MY WORTH
I no longer felt attached to the material possessions in my life. I like nice "things" but I knew more deeply that they do not define my worth as a human being. This now helps me resist the temptation to compare myself with others.

IT'S OK TO LET GO OF PAST PERSONAL FAILINGS
I seldom had difficulty forgiving other people, and now I was empowered to also forgive myself. What a relief! I even forgave myself for not having realized this sooner.

I LOVE THE PEOPLE IN MY LIFE
I was more appreciative of the people in my life, particularly those closest to me whom I would regularly take for granted. I can now listen to Harry Chapin's song, "Cat's in the Cradle" without getting emotional or upset.

UNACHIEVED GOALS ARE TEMPORARY
I gained an incredible sense of peace in regards to the goals I had not yet achieved in my life. Make no mistake, I was still driven to reach these goals, but not hitting goals did not throw me into a negative downward spiral the way it had before. This released me from any shame or guilt that usually surfaced when I fell short.

Suffice to say, the ah-ha realization brought an overwhelming sense of gratitude into my life and into my heart. At the time I was in graduate school, so I decided to research this topic.

It was kind of funny because I was studying in a business school and, in 2003, if you walked to the Dean's office and said, "I want do my research on the connection between gratitude and charitable giving," you would get a very strange look. Anyhow, that became my research, and through it I was privileged to have incredibly deep, meaningful conversations with generous people throughout my community. We talked about why they gave their time, why they helped others, why they gave their money, and why they served others.

Through the research, we built a model for the motivations for charitable giving, and found that gratitude was at the heart of generosity. The model for what motivates service and giving looked like layers of an onion: you just keep peeling back the layers of motivations until you uncover the most basic driving motivation. At the core, the motivation was a deep sense of gratitude for what these people had received in life.

My ah-ha moment radically challenged my beliefs about success. Up until that point, responsibility for success was an all-or-nothing thing. I believed success may involve some small degree of luck, but there was no in-between in terms of responsibility. You were either responsible or you were irresponsible. I subscribed to the adage, "The harder you work the luckier you get." I had to make sense of responsibility now that I had a radically different worldview. Responsibility for success, which I had previously evaluated from a binary yes-or-no perspective, transformed into a variable that existed across a continuum which now included the degree to which others contributed to my successes. Yes, I still had a role in my success, but it was never me alone. I could always find others who contributed. Some people I knew. Some I didn't know. Some were alive while others may have long since died. There were still others who I would fail to even recognize, not out of selfishness or ego, but because I just never thought of them.

The idea that our successes are intertwined with the contributions of others is not rocket science. I have discovered through the reactions I've received over the years that it is a thought-provoking idea. It flies in the face of popular culture and the mantras I carried about being self-made, as well as my strong sense of having an internal locus of control.

To make sense of this conundrum, I turned to Aristotle. They didn't teach us any philosophy in engineering school, so it was by accident that I tripped into him while reading about virtues. I was surprised to learn that Aristotle did not consider gratitude a virtue. But Cicero, who lived a couple hundred years after Aristotle, wrote, "Gratitude is not only the greatest of virtues, but the parent of all the others." My curiosity, driven by my conviction that gratitude must be a virtue, uncovered an argument that used Aristotelian logic to prove that gratitude is indeed a virtue, and an Aristotelian virtue at that.

Virtues are stable emotional traits or character states associated with excellence. They are generally social in nature and must have intrinsic value distinct from any external benefits. Every virtue sits at a midpoint on a spectrum. At both ends of the spectrum lie the extremes. For example, courage, as a virtue, sits at the midpoint between the extremes of cowardice and foolhardiness. Unfortunately, Aristotle didn't give us a user manual on virtues, because virtues are not about what one ought to do. Virtues are the path to a meaningful, happy life. Further, Aristotle believed that it takes experience and wisdom to know how and when courage veers from the midpoint and is no longer courageous.

The notion of virtues sitting on a spectrum, and the idea of gratitude as a virtue, helped me come to grips with my whole understanding of responsibility. Looking at gratitude, it sits at the midpoint between Ingratitude and Excessive Gratitude.

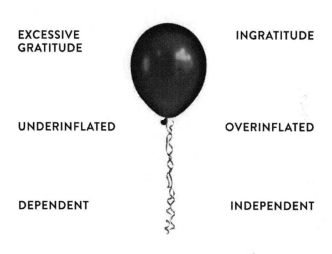

EXCESSIVE GRATITUDE   INGRATITUDE

UNDERINFLATED   OVERINFLATED

DEPENDENT   INDEPENDENT

Ingratitude fails to recognize the contributions of others and corresponds to an over inflated sense of self (ego)—highly egotistical—while excessive gratitude in the extreme fails to acknowledge one's own contributions, which is symptomatic of an under-inflated sense of self (ego)—a feeling of worthlessness. Somewhere in the middle lies a sense of self that is properly inflated. This balanced sense of self comes from a place of gratitude where you see your talents, gifts, and accomplishments more objectively for what they are and you see the connection with and contributions of others.

Building on the idea of connection with others, the overinflated sense of self aligns with the belief of being highly independent while the under-inflated sense of self aligns with the belief of being highly dependent. Miraculously, in the midpoint, we find interdependence.

In a world of interdependence, there are no victims and there are no heros. Everyone has unique worth. Successes and accomplishments are shared by the one who appears to have achieved them and the countless others who contributed in some way.

This explained it for me. It explained how responsibility is more than the binary extremes of responsible and irresponsible. As I look back at any success, how could I be completely responsible or completely irresponsible?

Having run four marathons, including Boston, which I qualified for in 3 hours 10 minutes, I had been of the mind that it was me who overcame my chubby adolescence and it was me who put in the miles of training and it was me who sacrificed so much time on long training runs in all kinds of crappy weather. And it was me who ran 3:10 to qualify for one of the most prestigious road races on the planet. My frame of reference for looking at my running was like a switch—either I was responsible or I wasn't.

Seven years after running Boston, I had the ah-ha moment which made me realize so clearly that, while without a doubt I played a huge part in my running success, clearly it was not my actions alone, nor was it my total, absolute responsibility. Others who crossed the finish line with me included my wife Lyn, who spent countless hours caring for our children, Nick and Stef, who both were under five years old, so I could complete the long training runs. She dealt with my moodiness as our busy lives collided with a heavy training schedule and sent me on my way to run because I was just so cranky. It included my friend Al—we trained for our first marathon together and we crossed the finish line side-by-side. Then there is Barrie, who inspired me by planting the seed inside of me that 26.2 miles was possible. My grandfather, Pappy, who gave me a special finisher's trophy that I still treasure, a symbol of his love and pride. My mom, who was a wonderful encourager—her letters and gifts made me feel loved and cared for. She gave me a special pair of running socks that I wore when I ran my first marathon and, in spite of the holes in them, I still keep them in my sock drawer some 30 years later. Boston was run in her honour for all that she did for me. My letter of gratitude at the time naturally flowed out of me and I held a vision of her in my mind throughout the race. This was especially effective as running grew difficult because it reoriented me from surviving to thriving in the midst of a grueling challenge.

In the summer of 2017, I took on a new project for my business. After considering a couple of peer learning forums, I decided to partner with MacKay CEO Forums. These forums bring together successful CEOs, business owners and executives with the sole purpose of helping them solve their biggest challenges and become better leaders. Launching two groups took a lot of work; there is no way I could have done it by myself. Attracting CEOs into a confidential forum such as this is not without its challenges. I was completely supported by Nancy and her team at MacKay. I had one-on-one coaching, weekly group calls, and a monthly call that brought together chairs from across the country. I had members and colleagues who opened their address books to recommend potential members. One member, Jonathan, brought me into his office with his assistant, and for an hour we went through his contact list name by name. When people ask me, "How did you do it?" I answer, "I'm like a turtle on a fence post." This usually gets a wrinkled brow, so I explain further. "If you're walking through a field and see a turtle propped on top of a fence post, you know one thing for sure. It didn't get there by itself." To be successful in this new venture, I knew I needed the support, so I took it. I worked hard that year, and so did many others. Together, working side-by-side, we launched two CEO groups in a new geographic market where the company had no name brand recognition.

As previously mentioned, my ah-ha moment left me feeling that it was as if my life was handed to me on a silver platter. This is the best way I can describe it. To be clear, this doesn't mean I sit back expecting that everything should be provided to me and I no longer have to do anything. Not at all. I still have a responsibility. In fact, when I truly embrace this silver platter belief, I will be overwhelmed with gratitude because it means I see my life as a gift. When you see your life as a gift, your whole life, the good, the bad, the ugly and all the crap that goes with it, there is only one appropriate response: gratitude. Nothing ignites gratitude within a leader more powerfully than seeing one's whole life as a gift. When you see your life as a gift, you lead from a place where you know that you have more than enough of what you need, and it profoundly reorients you from surviving to thriving.

Seeing everything as a gift is humbling and it can be very challenging. For example, our egos are constantly striving for external recognition and affirmation. I feel a temporary, immediate gratification when my ego wins, like when I drop a name of someone I know who is influential, or go on and on about all the things to do in a place I've visited. But the feeling quickly dissipates when I recognize I was doing it for my own attention and attaching my worth as a human to the people I know or places I've been. The desires of our egos are magnified by our individualistic society, which encourages us to stand out and to celebrate our individual accomplishments. In addition, society doesn't look fondly upon those looking for help. Our world interprets receiving help or asking for help as signs of weakness. Conversely, providing help is considered a strength. This is magnified for the stereotypical role associated with men. Remember, in a world of interdependence, there are no victims and there are no heroes. There are only people who are each uniquely gifted, who live in solidarity and support each other in their search for meaning, achievement and success. This is the essence of Grateful Leadership.

Having the humility to ask for help applies to big accomplishments like my engineering degree and equally to the smaller everyday issues we experience in our lives. For example, during the writing of this book, we were moving and needed to do a number of small renovations prior to our move. There was a little electrical, a bit of plumbing, some carpentry, some painting, some flooring and lots of cleaning. On top of this were the typical demands of daily living and work and purging stuff from our old house in preparation for the move. We hired packers and movers, but I figured we could save some money on the reno work as I could handle most of it. Lyn was pretty adamant that we should let professionals handle what they do best so that we didn't get overwhelmed. I was able to do a lot of the work, but there was no way I had the skill nor the time to do it all. My priority list was arranged based on my ability. The stuff I didn't know how to do was at the bottom and the easiest stuff was at the top of the list.

I enjoyed doing small jobs because I could see the fruit of my labour almost immediately. But I learned this approach was taking a toll on me. I was stressed because it was difficult to juggle the renos with the demands of my business, which was very busy at the time, and it was taking longer than expected to complete each little job. All the while, time was ticking. Lyn encouraged me to hire someone. Eventually and reluctantly, I said OK. Task by task, I said yes, and every time we brought in someone for a day or two, I felt an immense sense of relief. I was relieved both because I had one less "to-do" on my list and even moreso because I had the peace of mind knowing the job would be completed properly. The surprising aspect of this story is that this unfolded as I was writing this book, while I was writing about the idea of interdependence and the benefits of asking for help. This applies even if you're paying for the help.

Sometimes interdependence happens serendipitously. Peter is a professional colleague of mine through the Canadian Association of Professional Speakers. We speak on completely different topics, and we regularly meet for coffee to discuss our respective businesses and bounce ideas off each other. On Peter's prompting, our coffee meetings started after a professional development conference we attended. We didn't sign non-disclosure agreements. We just started meeting with the intention of helping one another. I can't speak for Peter, but these coffee meetings have been invaluable to me as they have helped me develop and expand intellectual property around gratitude.

There are formal and informal ways to experience the interdependence Peter and I provide each other. Regardless, it is wise to be intentional about building a network of supportive people. It will serve you well. You can partner with a colleague or friend. You can find a mentor or hire a coach. If you'd like to experience interdependence in a group setting you can join a mastermind group or a peer learning forum. I've been chairing one for the last year with amazing results.

I look for people with similar values that have the simple desire to make a positive difference in the world. Whether it's for your work, sporting pursuits, family matters or a community initiative, you can find others who've been there and done it, and you can learn from them and they can learn from you. Like most people, I tend to think I don't have much to offer and downplay my need for help. So I'm working on it simply by being aware of this natural human tendency and to be as equally aware of and grateful for the strengths I have been gifted with.

As I introduce the first law of grateful leadership, it's important to remind ourselves that you have innate value in the unique person you are. The first law of grateful leadership is foundational to being a thriving leader. In fact, if you can't accept this law, it will be one of the biggest obstacles to experiencing genuine gratitude and it will continually impede your ability to be a thriving leader and live a meaningful, purpose-led life.

FIRST LAW OF GRATEFUL LEADERSHIP

NO ONE IS SELF-MADE

IMPLICATIONS FOR YOU:
All of your successes, no matter how big or how small, are the result of your efforts and the efforts of countless individuals, some known to you and some unknown. Most frequently, the unknown far outnumber the known.

Acknowledging the contributions of others to your success is foundational to thriving. This first law can be a very difficult principle to accept because of the human ego and its desire for recognition.

ASK YOURSELF THE FOLLOWING QUESTIONS:

Which parts of my life do I see as gifts?

What have been my ah-ha moments?

Where am I most of the time on the dependence—interdependence—independence scale? Why might that be?

Are any of my values due for a time-out?

What are some of my biggest accomplishments, and who played a key role in these accomplishments?

KNOWING WHAT I KNOW, WHAT DO I TAKE AWAY FROM THIS CHAPTER?

CHAPTER 2

THE FOUR MINDSETS OF LEADERSHIP

I WAS SITTING IN Keith's office, crying. I felt lost. Totally and utterly lost. As a 41-year-old man, crying in front of someone didn't bother me. It was uncomfortable, but I didn't interpret crying as a sign of weakness. On the contrary, I interpret vulnerability as a strength.

Keith was my business coach. He asked insightful questions and challenged how I thought about the work I do and the way I show up in life. I can still remember the initial conversation with my boss, Robbie, who suggested executive coaching would likely be a game changer for me and recommended Keith.

I was excited about it. However, had it been six or seven years earlier, I would not have been. Previously, I had disdain for Keith. In the mid 1990's, he was the HR consultant hired to facilitate the laying off of 600 of my colleagues at Nova Scotia Power. Up to that point, I had thought I'd spend my entire career there. While Keith was not involved in the front end of the corporate restructure, his company handled all the terminations and transfers. As the lay-off deluge was about to begin, all of the "safe" managers were called into a meeting at the convention centre and were given our lists. My manager had already been let go, so I was feeling anxious and angry. Keith was centre stage at the meeting. I saw him as an ambulance chaser, cashing in on the misfortune of my friends and colleagues. At the time, I couldn't see that his work helped ensure that people were terminated with dignity and respect. While I'm sure there were exceptions, today I'm confident his influence over the process minimized the number of disrespectful layoffs. Still, I had no time for this grim reaper, and I saw him as small and opportunistic. I was one of the youngest managers in the company and, as a result of the restructuring, I would be returning to an engineering role. I was not happy about that.

But life goes on, and three years later I was on a senior leadership retreat where, for two days, the facilitator was none other than the grim reaper himself, Keith. Over the next 48 hours, I got to know Keith. He was vulnerable. He didn't claim to have all the answers. He challenged every person in the room, including my boss, who was the person who had hired him. Keith wasn't doing this retreat for the money. He got paid, I'm sure, but he was there to help people grow, and he was not going to let his ego or anything in his interests get in the way. So many people, me included, say what we think people want to hear. Not Keith. This man opened my eyes to the true person he was and he helped me grow as a leader and discover how quickly we can revert to survival modes of thinking when we feel threatened. Survival is truly a horrible place to lead from.

Before returning to Keith's studio office with me in tears, let's go back to my very first coaching visit. I would meet Keith at his house. When I walked into the studio, I immediately felt the calm. Maybe it was the earth-tone colour of the room, maybe the Asian artwork, maybe the sound of water bubbling over rocks in the vertical water fountain. I don't know, but it was calming. By this point we knew each other because of the group work we did together, so I decided that this was the time to share with Keith the first impression I had of him. "Keith, there's something you need to know."

"What is that Steve?"

"Well, my first impression of you was not positive. You probably don't even remember meeting me. I was one of a couple hundred managers at Nova Scotia Power when the big layoff happened in '95. As far as I was concerned, you were there profiting off the misfortune of my friends and colleagues. If you would have told me then that I would be coaching with you today, I would have bet the farm and family against you."

He smiled.

I went on. "Keith, I have the utmost respect for you. I realize now that the reaction I had when I first met you says more about me than it says about you. And besides, I was wrong and I'm glad I was wrong."

He was very non-judgmental and could quickly meet people where they were. "Thank you for sharing that story with me, Steve. I don't often come across as greedy and I'm glad we've been able to work together since. I'm even more excited about working with you in the future."

As I drove out the driveway, we had our coaching plan in place, and I had my first piece of homework around skills and values, but perhaps more than anything, I remember his promise: "We have our plan and we'll meet every two weeks, but I'm here for you. If you need to talk to someone, at any time, pick up the phone and call. I'll be here."

I never thought I'd take him up on that offer.

It was summer. I took a vacation day to create a long weekend. I had planned to spend about 30 minutes working on my goals in the morning before launching into a fun weekend. I've had goals for a long time and Keith helped me refine my process for building and working toward them. As I was pondering my goals at this time, I struggled to see the future. I could feel myself sink into a rut. I was replaying in my mind what I had been saying to myself in the weeks and months leading to this day. "You're no good. What difference are you making in the world? What's your purpose? Why are you here?" From the outside, it looked like I had it all (family, career, health, you name it) but I felt I was drifting. I said out loud, "You must have a purpose!" and started crying. I knew at that instant it was time to call Keith. He answered the phone and said, "Come on over."

He gave me a hug as I walked in. "What's up?"

I explained the hopeless feeling I had. "While I like what I'm doing, it feels like I'm drifting. It's as if I'm in the middle of the Atlantic Ocean in a boat without oars, no sail and no power. I felt I was drifting aimlessly, tossed by the sea. I know I have a purpose but I don't know what it is." As envy engulfed me, I told him, "In the last three weeks alone, I've spoken with two friends and each of them said to me, 'Steve, I'm doing exactly what I've been put here for.' Damn it, Keith, I want that!" I wanted it so badly, I remember salivating when they told me. In fact, I still salivate when I think back to those conversations.

Keith's response was profound. "At least you know."

"What do you mean, at least I know?" I quipped.

"At least you know, Steve. Do you know how many people out there don't even realize they have a purpose? At least you know you have a purpose. Don't worry. It will come."

That one line immediately shifted my perspective. It took what felt like the weight of the world off my shoulders and I felt very much at peace. All he did was help me find the good in my situation and reorient me from a survival mindset toward a thriving mindset. Knowing I had a purpose was a wonderful gift I hadn't seen. I was focused on the negative, which got a stranglehold on me and threw me into survival mode. It happens so easily.

While my purpose did not appear clearly for another two or three years, eventually it did surface, and while I was waiting, I knew it would come. This enabled me to thrive while I waited, even before I knew what it would be, which was very beneficial to my life and happiness. The purpose I found draws heavily on my skills and background life experience and it is to fulfill my dream: one billion happier people. We achieve that dream by bringing gratitude into people's lives so they can experience a thriving life. It is my hope that this book will contribute to a happier, more loving world with greater solidarity and unity.

Looking back, I realize during this time in my life, I was operating predominantly in what we call Striving Mode; occasionally I sunk into Surviving Mode.

LEADERSHIP IN A NUTSHELL

Leadership is a huge topic. There are many philosophies and models for leadership. If you ask 50 people to describe leadership in one word, you'll get many different answers and likely a few duplicate responses. Call it what you want, but the primary way I look at and think of leadership is in regard to the ability to influence. That influence obviously extends to others but also includes influence over self. Leadership lives in every corner of human existence. You find leadership in business, friendships, communities organizations, sports, government, NGOs, the military, you name it.

It is my core belief that everyone is a leader. Everyone,

regardless of position. I don't care if you are the CEO of Coca-Cola or you're babysitting an eight year-old down the street, you are a leader. Whether or not anyone is following is a measure of one's effectiveness as a leader, but everyone is a leader. We easily recognize the positional leaders in organizations and politics but, while usually obvious to the external observer, often people don't see themselves as leaders. For example, leaders are people who stop on the street to ask a homeless person about what they will eat that day; leaders are mothers who lend a hand to assist their daughters in raising their children; leaders are the most junior people in an organization who rally their co-workers to clean up the street outside the office on a Friday lunch break; leaders are people who volunteer their time in the community, whether they are knitting toques or raising millions of dollars. These people are all leaders.

The 10 Laws of Grateful Leadership cut across all boundaries. They apply within each and every realm of leadership regardless of the situation. You'll find these laws presented using a simple model that illustrates what we know to be true about leadership. I will spare you the distraction of citing reference upon reference that is typical of an academic work. This book is meant to provide a simple, practical approach to leadership that is accessible to anyone. The ideas in this book have been distilled from 12 years of research and professional practice in the field of gratitude. The 10 laws are not intended to be the alpha and omega of leadership. Quite the opposite, in fact. These laws offer a narrow and deep glimpse into leadership so that you can apply them and be a more effective leader regardless of who you are attempting to influence or what you want to bring about through your leadership.

The subject of leadership is important because, now more than ever, the world needs leaders who are thriving.

Too often leaders find themselves struggling, snarled in an endless busyness that leaves them feeling they are barely surviving. Their energy is consumed by this struggle, which stalls the leader's cause and hinders the ultimate needs of humanity. The more leaders thrive, the more humanity will thrive and, in my opinion, we need more of that.

The journey from surviving to thriving is not easy. As you'll see, it is very simple, but if you've come here looking for easy answers, you've got the wrong book. And simply understanding what it takes to go from surviving to thriving is not sufficient. Knowing is not enough. You have to actually do the work. You have to experience and practise the simple ideas contained in The 10 Laws of Grateful Leadership. It is not enough to just intellectually know the laws—no matter how well you understand them. "Knowing" is the lowest level of commitment. You must embrace these laws and they will continually orient you and reorient you toward thriving leadership, a journey you are on for the rest of your life. Don't be too hard on yourself, and enjoy it.

HIERARCHY OF LEADERSHIP

While there are many ways to look at leadership, we will examine the mindset of the leader within a hierarchy. Your mindset comes from your established attitudes and beliefs and it directly influences how you make sense of the world and dictates how you show up as a leader. This hierarchy enables people to self identify their level in the hierarchy and it clearly illustrates the challenge many people face as they try to break free from the unending struggle of survival. We call it the Hierarchy of Leadership, and the hierarchy goes from Surviving to Thriving. The hierarchy draws on my years in professional practice along with the many leaders I've observed first hand in my 40 years in the workforce.

Before we define and examine each of the four mindset levels within the hierarchy, it's important to note that you don't have to match every single characteristic associated with each level. In fact, you may be at a point between levels or, depending on the day, you may switch from one level to another. The bottom line is that there are exceptions, so you don't have to perfectly match the definition to understand where you sit on the Hierarchy of Leadership.

SURVIVING

Surviving is drudgery. It's like your world is a battleground. It's very lonely, even though people are all around. You feel overwhelmed and just can't seem to get to your priorities and, when you do, it seems like another one or two priorities get added. You suffer from poor sleep and don't pay attention to what you eat. Exercise would help relieve your stress, but you never exercise; there's no time and, if there were time, you'd want to just relax. When you look at others, it seems like everything is stacked against you and what you're trying to achieve. It is hard to muster up the energy to move forward, and it seems that you're constantly crushed by financial pressures and plagued by a myriad of challenges that never seem to end.

STRIVING

Striving is hard work. You are driven to succeed but there's seldom enough time in the day to get to everything, let alone work on your priorities. You find this exhausting, and at times you feel burnt out. You say you get enough sleep, but deep down know you're fooling yourself. You know what you should be doing when it comes to exercise and nutrition, but you just don't have the time. You've got goals, but you're frustrated because you're not making anywhere near your desired progress, and when you look at what others are doing, you feel like you should be doing better than they are. You hate being unable to spend quality time and quantity time with family and friends or on the fun things you used to always have time for. Financial pressures and other life challenges regularly determine what you can and cannot do. You truly know and believe there is more to life, although there are days it just doesn't feel that way.

ARRIVING

Arriving is a good place to be. You're generally satisfied in all areas of your life, but the feeling doesn't last—it's intermittent. This is also true with family, friends, and doing the fun things where time just flies by without noticing—you've got it, but not as much as you'd like. You're regularly achieving your goals in all areas of your life, have no serious financial challenges, but are easily frustrated by others who you feel don't deserve the success they've attained. You're generally satisfied with the balance of exercise, sleep and nutrition, feeling that, for the most part, it works. There are times you feel your life is controlled by others and the best use of your energy is spent on the many challenges you face, rather than on the things that bring you joy and happiness. Some days you feel like you've reverted to striving or surviving.

THRIVING

Thriving is where it's at. The world is your playground and you are very satisfied with all aspects of your life. You lead a meaningful, purpose-led life and compare yourself only to the aspiration of who you want to become. Family and friends are important, as evidenced by the amount of time you choose to spend with them. And when you're with them, your mind is with them and not distracted. You don't apologize for the time spent on hobbies and fun activities that bring you joy. While you may or may not be wealthy, financial pressures are virtually non-existent. You recognize your interdependence with the people around you by contributing with your unique gifts to those in your community, be it down the street or across the planet. You have lots of energy and enjoy optimal health because you adhere to proper sleep, diet and exercise. You're not a health fanatic, you've just figured out that healthy living doesn't have to be a chore, because it isn't. You still have lots of challenges, but you do not let them define you, nor get in the way of achieving your goals. You're busy, but you control your schedule, not others.

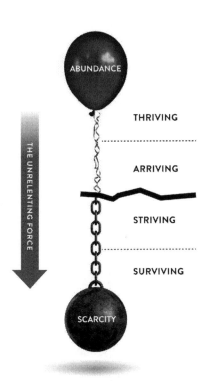

The Hierarchy of Leadership

Where do you spend most of your time? If you haven't already plunked yourself on the hierarchy, do so. Be honest with yourself. Is this where you want to spend most of your time? While the epiphany will come later in the chapter, consider for a moment those you lead: where are they on the hierarchy?

THE INVISIBLE BARRIER

There's a menacing invisible barrier that keeps most people stuck in the struggle of scarcity. This barrier exists whenever you let your guard down by losing sight of a belief that you know to be true. It's a simple belief, too. The belief is, "you are worthy and have much to be grateful for." The barrier isn't that you don't believe you have much to be grateful for, the barrier is that you lose sight of it, you forget. The barrier disappears when you consciously hold the belief. The barrier can't be seen, but it continually influences your mindset and the way you think, feel and act. When are you most at risk of letting your guard down and having the barrier keep you in survival mode? Is it when you get in an argument with your spouse, or a loved one experiences a health challenge, or when you are disciplined at work, or you lose a major client, or you get cut off in traffic? Any of these everyday occurrences can cause you to drop your guard and fall into surviving. One of the greatest challenges in keeping your guard up is that unless you are consciously on the lookout, you are completely unaware of the barrier and the impact it has on you. Fish aren't aware they are in water, humans aren't aware we are in air, and your heart beats without your brain consciously having to tell it to. The barrier will appear on its own the moment you let your guard down. It's as if you're operating on auto-pilot. I've heard it argued that low self-awareness is a good coping mechanism because having one less thing to worry about (like keeping your guard up against the barrier) makes life easier. However, when it keeps you stuck in a vicious cycle of surviving, low self-awareness is hardly worth it.

You will face many challenges in life; if you are unaware of the broader context of your situation, it becomes easier to adopt a victim mentality and conclude we're helpless, destined for more misery. In order to get unstuck from surviving, there are practical, simple steps anyone can do. The process begins with a simple choice to believe that you are worthy and have much to be grateful for, which opens the door to abundance. This prepares you to start looking for the good in your life and this alone will reorient your mindset from surviving to thriving. Don't worry. There are four simple, concrete habits, which we will cover later in the book.

THE UNRELENTING FORCE

For those who have known what it's like to thrive but today find themselves in survival mode, it's likely the result of the unrelenting force that pushes you down into survival mode. This force is composed of two unrelenting, smaller forces. The first is the human tendency to focus on the negative, which is known as negativity attribution bias. I like the way Dr. Rick Hanson describes it: "Our brains are like teflon to positive and velcro for negative." We'll talk more about this force in the next chapter, but the relentless force is constantly pulling you down. So you must constantly work on your leadership. Advance it and grow it, because the moment you stop, you start reverting to survival mode as the unrelenting force carries you downward on the Hierarchy of Leadership.

The second component of the unrelenting force is adaptation. When someone gets a raise, they are happy today, and for some time feel they have plenty. Wait three months, and suddenly their wages are no longer enough. They've adapted. Adaptation is another human trait that continually tugs at you pulling you down to surviving.

Remember, leadership goes beyond being the boss at work. It is critical to reinforce that your leadership is being tested in every moment—even when you least suspect you're expected to be a leader. Here are a few examples of everyday leadership that reoriented my mindset toward thriving leadership:

WORK

It was later in my career at Nova Scotia Power, and the company had decided to share the results of an employee survey. They wanted to demonstrate commitment from the top. Each Vice President was charged with presenting the results to the various work groups. The day my department got our debrief, our Vice President was out of town with another group. He had the majority of employees under his responsibility, making it impossible for him to attend every session for his division. So another Vice President, Murray, who had joined the company only months earlier, presented the results on his behalf.

As we were getting our coffee and settling in before the presentation started, Murray announced, "Sorry, but I have to leave early and may not be here to answer all your questions."

"Typical!" I thought to myself. "The leadership in this company cares no more about these results than they do if I got hit by a train." I was so mad I didn't even notice if my colleagues were upset by Murray's lack of regard for our team. I'm not sure if Murray noticed my crossed arms as he opened the session.

"Welcome. Thank you for taking time out of your day for the results of the employee survey. Hopefully you'll be able to provide some considered thoughts when you see the results. I mentioned I have to leave early. I'm sorry, but I do have to leave in 45 minutes to accompany one of my children to a very important medical appointment. Don't get me wrong, this survey is important to me, but I hope you'll understand that my family is more important to me. I would hope your family is more important to you, too."

I don't remember anything he said after that. I couldn't believe it. I had pegged Murray as a callous self-interested executive who couldn't care less about the rank and file in the company. Boy, was I wrong, and his stock skyrocketed in my mind that day.

Notice how the ever-present unrelenting force showed up without me even realizing it? I had pre-judged Murray and pushed my mindset down into survival mode. However, Murray's vulnerability changed how I saw him. His opening remarks were able to get me reoriented from a surviving mindset toward a thriving one.

PERSONAL
Early in our marriage, while still in college, we were at friend's house for dinner. The couple, Barrie and Alice, were about ten years older than us, and they treated us to a beautiful dinner. As a college student, I always loved dinners out. That night, we talked about running, because I had only started running a few years earlier, but Barrie had been running for quite some time. What I didn't know was that he had run marathons, which I discovered when I saw his finisher's certificate on the wall. I remember, as clear as it was yesterday, saying, "Wow Barrie, you ran a marathon. I always wanted to run a marathon, but there's no way I could ever do it."

Without skipping a beat, Barrie said, "Yes, you can. You can do it." For some strange reason, I believed him. I didn't start training for a marathon for another couple of years, but when I did, I teamed up with one of my best friends, Al. We trained for 10 months, through the cold depths of a Canadian winter and the humidity of a seacoast summer. Race day was a cold, wet Nova Scotian fall day. It was exhausting. It was painful. We were covered in blood from chafing—legs, arms and chest. It was not pretty, but it was an extremely emotional moment as the two of us crossed the finish line side by side. I later qualified for the Boston Marathon in the open division. This is something I had only ever dreamed of and never believed would ever happen to me. When I ran Boston, I was 32 years old and in the best physical shape of my life. I finished Boston in three hours and 25 minutes, placing 3003 out of about 10,000 runners. My children were quick to point out that in order to win my age classification, I would have had to run in the women's over 60 division.

Barrie made me believe something I thought impossible. He turned my mindset from impossible to possible, and in the process, pulled me upward from striving to thriving.

FAMILY

God bless her soul, my mom never complained. It wasn't because she didn't have a good reason; she had plenty of reasons. One of her ailments was a bad hip. It was very painful and eventually it was replaced when she was in her fifties. The operation wasn't successful, so she had another, and then, because of an infection, they had to remove the second prosthetic hip completely, send her home for six months without a hip, and then bring her back for a third, which lasted the rest of her life.

I remember one day, probably around month five with

no hip. She was in her chair. I asked, "How are you doing Mom?"

"Great, Sweetie, how about you?"

"Really? For five months you haven't been able to get up or go out and you're great?"

"Don't worry about me. I'm fine. Everything happens for a reason, Stephen."

As I look at Mom's descendants, my siblings and Mom's grandchildren, there isn't a complainer in the bunch. She left an indelible impact on everyone. She never told anyone, "Do not complain." She led by example. But if you did complain, you usually got her stock line, "Everything happens for a reason." More broadly, Mom's positive role modelling illustrates how leaders inspire lasting influence. She did not graduate from high school, yet she knew this essential leadership principle.

COMMUNITY

In late 2013, two friends of mine, Alex and Bill, were at a business networking event, and as people were giving their updates, one woman said, "We just started this group called 100 Women Who Care Halifax. We get 100 women to each bring $100 and then have three charities pitch an idea to us. We vote and whoever gets the most votes receives $10,000." Everyone at the meeting was quite impressed, and then she added, "I'm not sure if we could find five men who care." That got a good laugh, and it stuck with Bill and Alex.

A week later one of them asked the other, "Do you think she's right? Would men do the same?" So they invited about a dozen men together for breakfast, pitched the idea of 100 Men Who Give a Damn!—Halifax. There were no expenses, no red tape, the commitment was simple and easy, four hours and $400 per year. A group of us said yes, and our first cheque in early 2014 was for more than $27,000. Since then the group has raised almost $400,000 with zero expenses in five years. In addition, the "Give a Damn!" franchise has expanded to Ireland, The Cayman Islands, and to cities across Canada and the United States.

Bill and Alex were doubting yet hopeful. They resisted the temptation to do nothing and had the courage to test the idea on a group of colleagues. They cast a vision of how one person could multiply their philanthropy through collaboration with others and make a huge impact. Then they asked, "Who wants to join us?" This is thriving leadership. No sticks, no fear, no guilt. Just a simple invitation.

Within the Hierarchy of Leadership framework (discussed earlier in the chapter) lies an epiphany. Leadership is about influence, so as you dig deeper into the implications of the various leadership mindsets throughout the hierarchy, you'll find the second law of grateful leadership.

SECOND LAW OF GRATEFUL LEADERSHIP

The mindset of those you lead will be at or below your mindset

IMPLICATIONS FOR YOU:

As a leader (remember, everyone is a leader), you are the high water mark in every relationship, be it personal or professional. You cannot expect those you lead to operate with a mindset that is at a level that is higher than yours. If you are in a position of formal leadership and someone under your leadership has a mindset that is above yours, don't try to fool yourself that you're leading them. They won't follow you, just as you wouldn't follow someone who's mindset is below yours. It is your responsibility as a leader to set the example of leadership and model it in all you do. If you hold a formal leadership role and are responsible for others' development, you need to also help your leaders understand this law so those they lead can thrive.

As a leader, you want to help people believe they are worthy and have lots to be grateful for. This prevents the invisible barrier from holding them prisoner in survival mindset and opens the potential for them to thrive.

ASK YOURSELF THE FOLLOWING QUESTIONS:

Who comes to mind when I think of a thriving leader and what do they do that makes them thrive?

Where do I spend most of my time in the surviving to thriving hierarchy?

How do I see the unrelenting force show up in my life?

What can I do to be continually oriented toward a thriving mindset?

Who do I need to remind they are worthy and have lots to be grateful for?

KNOWING WHAT I KNOW, WHAT DO I TAKE AWAY FROM THIS CHAPTER?

CHAPTER 3

THE SOLUTION

As my 13 year career at a great company was coming to an end, it felt like I was in a tailspin. Close friends, family and especially colleagues at work said, "Steve, how are you handling this? I can't believe you're so positive." It was all a façade, and apparently I was doing a good job of making it look like I was thriving. Just prior to the tailspin, it felt as though I was at a high point in my career. And then came corporate changes, which included my boss, a Vice President, voluntarily leaving the company. I was seconded to a special project team, so I fell into a limbo, which meant I needed to come up with a plan for my future in the company. I had conversations with many senior people, and I was beginning to feel very anxious about whether there would be a future for me at the company I so dearly loved. Although I was at peace with leaving, I became ever more anxious about the conversations I was having with different managers and members of the executive team. So anxious, that I did something I never had done before in my life: I started documenting every conversation I had. I printed every email related to career discussions. And I kept all documentation at home in a binder. I didn't trust leaving it at work, because if I was laid off, there would be no guarantee that I would be able to get it. This would be my evidence and I wasn't willing to risk losing it.

I was unable to create a new position that would be of value in the company, and there were no other positions at my management level open at the time. The options were dwindling. If I wanted to stay in the company, I would have to take a demotion to a lower level job. They would hold my compensation based on my previous role, but I would not be able to advance my pay grade. This started another round of conversations about another option, exiting the company. I explained how the demotion would look like constructive dismissal, and at this stage in my career, it would be jeopardizing to me. We discussed two options: accept the transfer, which in my mind was clearly a demotion, or reject the transfer and trigger a severance package. Lyn and I had agreed that it was time for me to leave the company and that a fair severance package would be sufficient to protect the family while I searched for new employment. So I rejected the transfer and asked about next steps on the severance. The person I was dealing with said he'd get back to me because up to this point everything was a verbal agreement, other than my documented notes. I called Kevin, the manager in the department I was to be transferred to, and declined his offer. Kevin was a friend—we had worked together previously—and he was surprised, as he knew I had no other options in the company. Driving home, I felt mixed emotions. Peace about the decision, hope for the future and sad for what felt like the loss of 13 years of friendships and contribution.

I wasn't prepared when I opened my email the next morning. I was shocked. I could feel the flood of cortisol through my body and the accompanying stress that squeezed my chest. I was in panic mode. A new senior manager met with me and explained that severance was not an option for me and he wasn't sure where I would have gotten that impression. He gave me one last chance. He said, "Either take the job transfer or quit. And if you want the job, you'll have to call Kevin and ask him if he'll still have you. And we need to know today."

There was no way I could quit. Our financial situation would crumble within months. We had just started building a new house; our kids were ten and nine. Reluctantly, I called Kevin and asked for the job transfer and I started the next week. I spent all evening documenting what happened. It was hard to control my anger. Lyn was furious.

Kevin was a delight to work with again. I had no hard feelings against him nor those I worked with, but I couldn't stay. I started looking for another job, and six months later I found one and resigned. Kevin and his boss, John took me to lunch during my last week. They expressed disappointment it didn't work out but weren't surprised I left. They asked, "Was it for more money?"

I lied. "Yes." I didn't have the courage to tell them I took a 25% pay cut in the new job.

For six years I worked in that new job, and then, in 2007, I left to start my gratitude company. The whole time my binder of notes documenting my last few months at Nova Scotia Power sat in my file closet with all my business materials. I didn't notice it every time I went in the closet, but came across the binder every few months when I went digging for something. It was three or four years into the gratitude business when I saw it for the last time.

As I looked at the white binder and thumbed through the loose-leaf pages, all written in different coloured ink, I recalled how I thought the binder was my source for power and control. I wanted to hold on to it in the event that someday I might want to bring in a lawyer to force the company to cough up the compensation I felt I so rightfully deserved. Then it dawned on me. "I don't possess this binder. This binder possesses me!" I was in survival mindset. I thought, "How could I expect to be effective in teaching grateful thriving leadership while I'm clinging to past hurts and unable to get past them?"

I rolled my chair over to the shredder and in less than five minutes, I was free! The binder was gone. I forgave everyone involved, in particular, those I felt aggrieved by. I let it go. It was like the scene from *The Shawshank Redemption* when Andy emerges from the quarter-mile sewage pipe to complete his escape from the prison. If you recall, he was cleansed of the sewage by a downpour of torrential rain. Ridding myself of that binder was like unloading a burden, and it immediately shifted me from a scarcity mindset to an abundance mindset; it reoriented me toward thriving. Since shredding that binder and forgiving the characters who played the villains (at least in my mind), I've been able to re-establish business relationships with them. While they are business relationships, they are rooted in dignity, and not limited to the utilitarian value that may or may not be exchanged.

While I was in survival mindset I could only see the negative crap in this situation. This provided me a self-fulfilling prophecy of doom and gloom. Once I let go of my expectations and feelings of entitlement and replaced my perspective with gratitude, I was able to thrive. Since this time, these same characters who I thought were villains have hired me, referred me, supported causes I believe in, and helped my business. Had you told me that all these positive outcomes would happen while I was in surviving mode, I would have laughed at you.

WHY GRATITUDE?

We need a way to move through the invisible barrier that keeps people stuck struggling in survival mindset. To recap, the invisible barrier is a block in our mindset that appears when we aren't consciously aware that we are worthy and have lots to be grateful for. When you believe you're worthy and have much to be grateful for, it opens the possibility for abundance, and when you start practicing gratitude, you notice things you hadn't previously and this moves your mindset upward. We each have a natural tendency to see good or bad or neutral. Two people can find themselves in the same situation and make sense of their situations in very different ways. Possibly in opposite ways. One may see fear (scarcity) and the other may see opportunity (abundance). It really depends on the person's mindset.

The factor that has the greatest influence on whether you experience scarcity or abundance is your mindset. As previously stated, we need to make sure we remove the invisible barrier which automatically appears when you let your guard down and forget to hold the belief that "you are worthy and have much to be grateful for." While it may be difficult to believe, being grateful is the skill that has the greatest impact on calibrating your perspective and reorienting your mindset from surviving toward thriving. Additionally, gratitude overcomes the unrelenting force that continually pulls you downward to surviving.

Martin Seligman, the founder of Positive Psychology, developed a model for human flourishing (think thriving) which is rooted in 24 positive character strengths. These are character strengths like hope, openness, bravery, and honesty. One of his colleagues, Barry Scott Kaufman, mused, "24! There's no way I can work on 24 strengths. What if I can work on just one? What is the single character strength that is the best predictor of a flourishing life?" So, as part of a larger study on introversion that involved more than 500 participants, he did an analysis on what is the best predictor of human well-being. He found that only gratitude and love of learning independently predicted well-being, and the single best predictor was gratitude.

To more deeply understand the effect gratitude has on your perspective, a thriving mindset and why it is so critical for leadership, we need to look at what we call The Cycle of Leadership Influence.

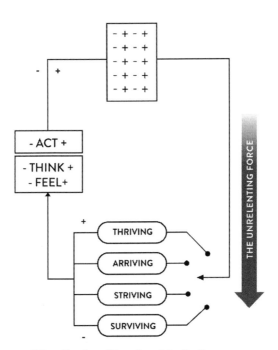

The Cycle of Leadership Influence

Quite simply, the world around us consists of events, situations, and circumstances that are either positive, negative, or neutral. When you observe and take in your surroundings, everything gets filtered by your mindset. If your mindset is negative or biased toward surviving, you will notice more of the negative in the environment around you, you will have a very difficult time seeing the positive and you will even make sense of positive events in a way that is negative.

Every input into your brain is processed into thoughts and feelings. Both your thoughts and feelings can be positive, negative, or neutral. While psychologists have models that explain the cognitive, affective, and behavioural aspects of human existence, my simple engineering model looks at your brain as a black box. This black box quickly applies mental calculus to your thoughts and feelings, which ultimately causes you to act. Your actions are external and therefore influence the surrounding environment in either a positive, negative or neutral manner. The cycle repeats again.

The most important element in The Cycle of Leadership Influence is the filter, which is your mindset. It can be set to any of the four levels of leadership on the Hierarchy of Leadership: Surviving, Striving, Arriving, or Thriving.

If your filter is set to surviving, you will notice more negativity, be more gloom-ridden as you process events and people and then behave more pessimistically, creating more negativity in your environment, and making it easier to notice that negativity. It's a vicious cycle that continually reinforces the survival mindset.

In contrast, if your filter is set to thriving, your mindset is biased toward positive perception, so you will focus more on the positive aspects in your environment, process them more optimistically and then act more constructively, creating more positive outcomes in your environment, thus making it easier to see more positivity in the world around you. This is a virtuous cycle that translates into a thriving mindset and more meaningful life.

Thriving is not about hedonistic happiness focused on one's self. While mainstream culture preaches "happiness is found in self and stuff," genuine happiness has nothing to do with either of these. In many ways, thriving has little in common with happiness rooted in pleasure. When you flourish and thrive, according to Martin Seligman, you possess and excel in four distinct higher order characteristics that characterize who you are and how you live.

LIFE SATISFACTION

You feel great about work, your health, and your personal relationships with family and friends. Your happiness is unwavering, deeply grounded in knowing who you are and what your role is on this planet. Your happiness is not a roller coaster ride of ups and downs dictated by feelings that shift based on whether your life circumstances are positive or negative.

GROWTH

You are growing and building lasting personal resources that will serve you well into your future. You know life is a journey and not a destination, therefore you invest in yourself. This might be through formal education and professional development or having the presence of mind to transform every challenge into a learning opportunity.

RESILIENCE

You are resilient and able to bounce back after setbacks. Challenges do not define you, nor do they control you.

GENERATIVITY

You are adaptable and function effectively when you're thrust into new or uncertain circumstances and situations.

BENEFITS OF GRATITUDE

No book on gratitude would be complete without some mention of the benefits of a grateful frame of mind. Each of these contribute to a thriving mindset. The science around gratitude continues to grow, and while researchers are still working to determine the cause-and-effect mechanism that gratitude plays, at the time of writing this book we know gratitude is connected to the following positive outcomes for Thriving Leadership:

PHYSICAL HEALTH

Grateful people age more gracefully and live longer lives. While they don't even realize it, they have superior cardiac functioning, and if something goes wrong with their hearts, they recover more quickly after serious heart surgery. They enjoy a lower risk of diabetes and they are sick less often, likely because they have a greater resistance to viral infections. Grateful people exercise more regularly and sleep more soundly, which are two critical factors to a healthy lifestyle. Gratitude appears to play a role both in the prevention of disease and in healing from disease.

MENTAL HEALTH

Perhaps the most coveted benefit of gratitude is the gift of happiness. Grateful people are happier all the time, even when crap happens in their lives. To the outsider it's inexplicable. The brains of grateful people produce more of the good brain chemicals and less of the troublesome brain chemicals, which means they are less likely to be depressed or experience feelings of hopelessness. They hold a more optimistic outlook on life, even when life deals them a rotten hand in the form of a medical diagnosis or any of a myriad of tragedies. Their superior mental resilience means grateful people are less likely to be anxious when they find themselves in crowded, unfamiliar places, less upset if they were to be laid off and better able to take it in stride when travel plans get derailed.

SOCIAL

Grateful people don't experience the same degrees of loneliness as others because they are more likely to have a wide network of strong relationships of people who support them and people they support. They gain as much strength from those they support as those they can count on. They are generous with their time, money and skills. They give generously to support causes and people in a way that aligns with their personal strengths and beliefs. Grateful people actually feel like they get more by being generous, but that's not why they are generous. Their generosity is genuine, whether it is spending time with a colleague who's suffered a setback at work, coaching the local kids' soccer team, sitting on a volunteer board or helping someone panhandling for change on the street.

PERSONAL

Grateful people are inclined to use "approach behaviours" that keep them moving forward and more likely to complete unpleasant tasks, which makes them more likely to achieve important life goals. Whether it's at the gym, on local trails or playing sports with friends, grateful people have habits that help them live life to the fullest. When they get up in the morning they feel refreshed and ready to go and have the energy and stamina to tackle whatever comes their way. Grateful people are less materialistic and much happier. Spending money makes grateful people happy when it's spent on an experience like dinner with friends, rather than on purchases like another new jacket.

NO MAGIC PILL

Although there are many benefits associated with gratitude, it should not be considered a magic pill. What I mean by this is, you actually have to do something with what you learn in this book. You can't simply read the book and think that having the knowledge of what it takes to be a Thriving Leader is sufficient. You need to make sense of how gratitude appears in your life and then you have to make it work for you. Gratitude is for experiencing, not merely understanding. For example, say you understood everything about coffee, how to grow and harvest it, how to roast it, how to blend varieties to produce different coffees and create unique flavours. You knew everything there was to know about coffee but you had never tasted coffee. Would that make you an expert at coffee? Hardly. You must experience coffee to truly understand coffee. Gratitude is similar: if you are to genuinely embrace gratitude you must experience gratitude through the ups and downs of everyday life.

Gratitude is also like laughter. If you consider laughter, you know what laughing is. You know how to laugh. You know that when something is funny you laugh, and when it's really funny, you laugh a lot more. Laughing just happens without any awareness of the psychological mechanism involved in humour. But here's the thing, and this applies even if you understand the systematic process by which humans find something humourous: if I tell you to laugh and expect you're going to laugh—genuinely laugh—we're fooling ourselves. For you to genuinely laugh, you need to experience something humourous.

Gratitude is not an intellectual exercise. I can't just tell you to be grateful and expect you'll be grateful, even if you have all the gratitude knowledge there is. You must make gratitude a practice and the more you do, the more you will experience gratefulness.

Like laughter, we can rest easy knowing that gratitude is easily accessible to anyone regardless of age, income, race or geography. In reality, all you need to do is ensure you don't let your guard down, and consciously hold on to the belief that "you are worthy and have much to be grateful for." This ensures the invisible barrier doesn't get in your way of thriving.

The science of gratitude is crucial to understanding its benefit as a fundamental leadership competency. However, this knowledge is quite separate from what you need to do to bring about a positive, growing, resilient, and grateful frame of mind.

There is only one way to truly learn about gratitude, the impact it can have on your life as a leader and how it can reorient you from surviving to thriving. You must experience gratitude. The more you experience it, the better you get at it. It is like you have a gratitude muscle, and like any muscle, if you don't use it, you lose it. You'll want to establish your own gratitude practice comprised of exercises and habits, which we'll get to later, that contribute to a more grateful frame of mind. Practicing gratitude takes effort because there are all kinds of competing demands on your time and priorities that get in the way. And whether you're practicing gratitude or not, the unrelenting force is continuously pulling you downward into survival mode.

While we have a fast growing body of scientific evidence in support of gratitude and using it to be a Thriving Leader, fortunately humanity did not wait for the evidence to mount before adopting gratitude into how we grew as societies.

My parents taught me to say thank you. I can only imagine this is on the heels of generation upon generation who raised their children to understand the importance of being grateful and thankful. I don't remember Mom and Dad setting this example, because it started at such a young age. But I see our daughter Stef teaching our grandson Max to say please and thank you, and I remember teaching both of our kids to say thank you. For Lyn and me as the leaders in our family, we really didn't think twice about why we were teaching this to our kids other than it seemed like the right thing to do and "It's good manners." There's a strong common sense argument to being grateful and now there's a lot of scientific data around gratitude that supports what our ancestors taught for generations. If you ignore gratitude as the foundation for your leadership, you do so at your own peril and risk constantly being dragged down into the struggle of survival mindset.

This story illustrates another example of how survival mindset did not serve me well and how the practice of focusing on positive qualities reoriented me to a thriving mindset. I pride myself in not talking about people behind their backs. In the late 1990's came an exception. It was Earl. He was loud and I considered him an arrogant know-it-all. Before I knew it, I was complaining about him to my colleagues at work and my friends at home. When I talked about him, it was not shared in a helpful way. I fell into spreading editorialized stories that reinforced my beliefs about Earl as I tried to convince others of his shortcomings. Fortunately, I realized what I was doing and I really didn't like it. I may have felt good momentarily when I poisoned someone else's view of Earl, but in no time, it would eat away at me. I talked to my friend James about it because I wanted to change what I was doing. I really didn't care that much about spreading what I believed to be true, but I was more concerned that I would begin talking about other people in my life. James said, "Pray for him." Most of my friends would not have told me to pray, but James is a priest. So I did. I prayed for him. I thought positive thoughts about Earl. I wished him success. I wished the best for his family and took an interest to learn the names of his children and wife. The results were amazing.

I don't know how Earl managed to change but he no longer was the schoolyard bully I had portrayed him to be. I grew to like and respect him. The fact of the matter is that Earl did not change. I changed. Instead of focusing on every one of Earl's faults I began to notice more and more of his strengths. I grew to appreciate him. We became colleagues and worked on a few projects together and were very effective when we worked together. When he left the company, I considered him a friend like the vast majority of the people I worked with. If you find yourself in a similar circumstance and are comfortable praying, then pray. If praying is not for you, then think positive thoughts. This changed my perspective filter and reoriented me toward a thriving mindset. It paid dividends quickly.

As we turn our attention to the third law of grateful leadership, we find a reassuring principle that is very unique to being grateful and is a mantra of the world's leading scientific expert on gratitude, Dr. Robert Emmons.

THIRD LAW OF GRATEFUL LEADERSHIP

THERE ARE NO SIDE EFFECTS TO DEVELOPING A GRATEFUL MINDSET

IMPLICATIONS FOR YOU:
Unlike most medications and pills that have negative side effects, you don't have to worry about anything bad or horrific happening as a result of being grateful. This mitigates any perceived risk you may have about being a grateful leader. Further, being grateful doesn't cost anything. Gratitude can only help you become a better leader. While there are no side effects, accepting the fact that your success is because of others, which comes from the First Law of Grateful Leadership, can be a hard pill to swallow because our egos like to think we are very important and self-reliant.

There is no evidence to suggest that you will be exploited or taken advantage of because you are grateful. That said, tragedies and situations in which someone is being exploited do not necessarily constitute a reason to be specifically grateful for. There are limits to what I can be grateful for. For instance, I'm not grateful for the death of my mom in 2013 but I can easily find good and find lots to be grateful for in the circumstances and events and people surrounding her death.

ASK YOURSELF THE FOLLOWING QUESTIONS:

What am I attached to, such that it possesses me?

When have I only been able to focus on the negative aspects of a situation? How did it serve me?

What is my perspective filter (i.e. mindset) most of the time—surviving, striving, arriving or thriving? What does this mean to me?

Do I truly believe that the reasons for my successes lie in the countless people that have supported me? Why?

Which benefits of gratitude are important to me?

KNOWING WHAT I KNOW, WHAT DO I TAKE AWAY FROM THIS CHAPTER?

CHAPTER 4

BUT IT'S THE WAY I'M WIRED

IT'S HARD TO BELIEVE that we can change our makeup as a person. In high school, I was introverted, shy and just trying to fit in. For my Grade 11 history class, each student was required to prepare and teach one class. There's no way I was going to speak in front of the class. I didn't want to look bad or be judged, and I wasn't comfortable being vulnerable in front of the class. I was pretty judgmental myself, thinking I was too cool to do something I thought was for the keeners and nerds. Heaven knows why I stayed in the class. The presentation was a very important part of the course and would account for 50% of our grade. As the term unfolded, student after student took their turn teaching.

When my turn came, Mrs. Hopkins invited me to the front of the room: "Stephen, as you know, today's your day. We're looking forward to it!"

I said, "I didn't prepare anything. I'm not doing it."

She couldn't believe it. "But you'll get a zero and you'll fail the course this term."

"I don't care. I'm not speaking in front of the class." In the end I did not teach my lesson and earned a zero. My fear of speaking was huge and I knew that would never change.

Five or six years later, I landed my first summer job as an engineering intern in Oshawa, Ontario with General Motors. On the first day, we learned that at the end of our summer internship, each of us would give a 20 minute presentation to the senior management team at the plant. My fear of public speaking had not abated, but there was no way I could duck out on this presentation the way I did in grade 11. The summer came and went. I got anxious whenever I thought about the presentation, but as expected the presentation came and went. No one died. No one was embarrassed. To the contrary, after the presentation, I felt incredibly alive and that I had achieved a huge accomplishment. As I sat in the boardroom that day, I realized two things: 1) in spite of being nervous, I actually enjoyed speaking to groups, and 2) I was good at it, at least in comparison to a bunch of other student engineers.

After I started working at Nova Scotia Power I found myself regularly speaking to groups as part of my job. Seldom a month passed that I didn't do a safety presentation or speak to a community group of some sort. I loved helping people find their penny-drop moments. The speaking and teaching ended up being one of the most rewarding parts of my job. It was hard for me to believe that not ten years prior I took an F in History because I was afraid to stand in front of an audience.

As my career progressed I started to consider professional speaking and I discovered the Canadian Association of Professional Speakers (CAPS). I couldn't believe it; there was a professional association, and they even had a chapter in my city. I shared my aspirations for speaking for a living with two close confidants, Robbie and Mike. Both of them gave well-intentioned advice. Essentially, they both said, "Bad idea. You'll never be able to make a living at it." I was a little hurt and more embarrassed for even suggesting the idea, so I buried it. Then, three or four years later, I had my ah-ha moment when I realized my life was handed to me on a silver platter. This was what led to my research, which eventually got me into my work with gratitude; the idea of speaking professionally resurfaced because ever more frequently I was being asked to speak about gratitude.

Four years later, my friend Peter persuaded me to join CAPS, which I did in 2010. Since then I have served as Chapter President for CAPS Atlantic, was elected to the CAPS National Board of Directors and in 2017, I was one of 47 people globally awarded the highest earned designation in professional speaking, The Certified Speaking Professional (CSP), awarded by the National Speakers Association. For comparative purposes, on average, more people summit Mount Everest in a single year than the cumulative number of people who have earned the CSP. I've spoken in community halls, church basements, penthouse boardrooms, schools, meeting rooms, hotels, resorts, auditoriums, convention centers, and lunch rooms. Speaking has taken me around North America from exotic destinations to mundane locales.

I'm not the most in-demand speaker on the planet, nor in the country, for that matter, but it's a far cry from Grade 11 history class. There is no question that I had a hard-wired fear of speaking and it wasn't going to change. It is the classic example of having a fixed mindset about who I was and what I could do. Fortunately I fell into the undesirable circumstances at General Motors that proved I was wrong. I could change, and while it took a few years, I did.

Limiting beliefs similar to my fear-of-speaking, left unchallenged, will extend into all areas of our lives and restrict our ability to change who we are and what we can do. Chances are you can relate to the fear of speaking even if you love the limelight. Regardless, maybe you grew up isolated without a lot of love, or maybe you didn't do well in school or maybe you are shy. Whatever it is, it need not define who you are and what you can do.

We each are blessed with gifts and natural tendencies. Gifts are the skills, aptitudes and abilities you possess, like being able to sing or solve a complex math problem. Natural tendencies are the way you are internally wired as a human being. One such tendency is your inclination to be either introverted or extroverted. One of these comes more naturally to you and you are more comfortable in that mode of being or action. But that doesn't mean you can't adopt the other style, although it will likely take some effort. For example, you may prefer to have a long conversation with just one person at a large social gathering, but you are fully able to step out of your comfort zone and have many different brief conversations with a lot of people, some whom you've never even met before. If the motivation or inspiration is big enough, you'll do it. As you do this unnatural activity more and more, you'll get better at it and it will become more natural to you. While it may never take the place of your natural tendency, you can adapt to this style. For me, I'm still an introvert, although few people would identify me as an introvert because I've worked very hard at intentionally spending time being more extroverted.

When it comes to gratitude, there are a few tendencies that can make you more predisposed to gratitude and more open to being a grateful leader. For example, if you are naturally optimistic, gratitude will come to you more naturally. You are also more predisposed to be grateful if you are female or if you are older.

While being a positive older lady might make it easier to have a grateful mindset and be a grateful leader, if that's not you, don't worry; you're not destined to a life struggling in survival mindset. You can still thrive. Be open to change like the introverted kid who refused to speak in history class, who later ended up speaking for a living because he was open to the possibility. Don't let your guard down. It begins by holding on to the belief, "I'm worthy and have lots to be grateful for."

Neuroscientists have discovered our brains continue to grow and evolve; this concept is called neuroplasticity. Your brain is not fixed and hardened like a stone, always the same, never to change. In essence this means your brain has the ability to be molded. To build and strengthen a thriving mindset, all we have to do is create new neural pathways that support new ways to think and act. While it sounds complex, it is a natural part of your human physiology and your brain will do it without you even asking, similar to your body's capacity to heal a cut on the back of your hand. Neuroplasticity underlies the process of learning to walk again after a serious accident; such patients rewire their brains.

In terms of gratitude, each of us has a natural set point toward being grateful. This is your default disposition to gratitude and is known as your Trait Gratitude. The higher your disposition to gratitude, the greater the instantaneous gratitude, known as State Gratitude, you will experience for any given circumstance. Ultimately, the more you develop your Trait Gratitude, the less time you'll spend surviving and more you'll spend thriving. State Gratitude is the moment-by-moment gratitude that ebbs and flows as your day unfolds.

No two people are alike. Your natural tendencies separate you from everyone else and make you the unique person you are.

When it comes to being a Grateful Leader, let's recap a few natural tendencies regarding our disposition to being grateful (Trait Gratitude):

- Optimistic people tend to be more grateful
- Spiritual and religious people tend to be more grateful
- Older people tend to be more grateful
- Women tend to be more grateful

Fortunately this is not cast in stone. You can be a young, pessimistic, non-spiritual male and still have a thriving mindset and lead a thriving life. The opposite is also true. Just because you have all the natural tendencies that would predict a high Trait Gratitude, doesn't mean you will automatically have a thriving mindset.

Regardless, because of the unrelenting force that is pulling you down from Thriving to Surviving, there's a tendency for our Trait Gratitude to erode if we don't do something to continue to build it. Unfortunately, this is the equivalent of your brain rewiring itself to being less grateful.

I've known Mark for a long time. From the outside he was always positive, confident and very spiritual. On the inside, he was like me. Fearful people would see him for who he really was. Uncertain he was worthy of living a thriving life. He was resigned, unable to change, and living as he always had. We reconnected at his wedding and he was intrigued by my work with gratitude. He quickly realized that, although he was optimistic, his optimism was superficial, because deep down he did not feel positive. He was trying the "fake it till you make it" mantra, but it just wasn't working for him, and the "faking it" was eating away at him. Because of the trust we share, he didn't think twice about starting down the gratitude path. Today, Mark credits gratitude and his new-found practice of making a gratitude list as the key to the transformation in his life. He's joyously made a career move that he previously was unable to consider because, like so many of us, he thought he didn't deserve it. He faced the same question many people face: "Is it OK to thrive, to have more and to live in abundance, when so many people barely have enough to get by?" While Mark is still growing his gratitude muscles, he is experiencing a new type of thriving in his life, and it is solely because he changed his mindset.

BEING PRIVILEGED

Being a straight, white, male comes with privilege—a lot of privilege. At least in North America, it is an unearned privilege because on balance, in 2019, everything is definitely easier for this group of people and relatively speaking, it has been easier for this group of people for a long, long time.

I have no right to tell you that you have privilege and that you should be grateful for all aspects of your life and that you need to see your life as a gift. While I believe this is true for every human on the planet, I can't proclaim it for you and I won't judge you if you don't see this truth for yourself. Heck, for 40+ years I didn't see it in my own life, so it would be a bit ironic if I was to be so judgmental. The core belief on which we base our gratitude practice, "I am worthy and have much to be grateful for" is essentially our "privilege."

If you don't acknowledge your privilege, you run the risk of confusing your lack of privilege with the reason you are only surviving. On the opposite end of the spectrum, it becomes easy to fabricate a connection between privilege and all who are thriving. This sort of victim mindset seldom serves anyone well. Again, this can be a difficult idea to embody when we witness so much suffering and oppression in the world, which at the same time stands in contrast to the unprecedented levels of wealth that exists in most of the western world. It is difficult to acknowledge privilege when life seems to deliver hardship after hardship, whether to your financial, health or family circumstances. And when you read the previous sentence about unprecedented wealth, did you include yourself in the group of people who possess "unprecedented wealth"? Most people do not see themselves as wealthy, but we know it to be true that if you're reading this book, it's likely that you should be included in that group who possess "unprecedented wealth." The average western world lifestyle is greater than that of royalty who would have lived about 100 years ago when the Titanic sailed. Shocking, but true.

Comparing, which we'll cover in more detail in Chapter 7, is harmful. And the person it harms most is the one doing the comparing: you. When we compare ourselves to others, it reinforces our beliefs about our own privilege and erodes our ability to see our wonderful unique giftedness. For a moment, let's assume that everyone has privilege. What privilege do you have? Where are you gifted?

As you think about your life, where have you been privileged? Places to look for privilege are far reaching: country of birth, time in history in which you live, gender, race, family support, educational opportunities, sports involvement, employment opportunities, living conditions, relationships, friends, the food on your table.

For quite some time now, I've felt it's as if I won the lottery of life. What about you?

I believe everyone has privilege. And comparatively speaking everyone has different privilege. Whether it is more or less really isn't the issue; the real issue is being able to see and acknowledge the genuine privilege you have. Just as you see the genuine gifts and talents you have.

BECOMING MORE GRATEFUL

While we will dive more deeply into the specific mechanics of how to develop a thriving mindset to become a Grateful Leader and how to remain a Grateful Leader, it comes down to habits. Habits are the automatic behaviours that influence the vast majority of daily action and determine the degree of success you experience in life. When a behaviour is automatic, it means you don't even think about it. You just do it. Habits can be good, or habits can be bad, depending on the behaviour. Because they are automatic, good gratitude habits are your best defense against the unrelenting force. So in relation to becoming a Thriving Leader, we've distilled all of the various gratitude behaviours down to four simple yet distinct habits. These habits take me between four and eight minutes per day. Most days I spend more time on them, easily double the time, but that's my choice.

Over time, as you use and develop your own gratitude habits, your brain gets rewired and you increase your disposition toward gratitude (Trait Gratitude), making you more susceptible to seeing the good in the world around you and increasing the frequency and intensity of your gratitude feelings (State Gratitude).

The easiest way to experience gratitude in all aspects of your life is to see your life as a gift. Yes, every aspect of your life as a gift. This comes easier to some people than others. For instance, my story from the judgemental oldest of five, to engineer, to gratitude teacher all hinged on an ah-ha moment.

Many people have asked me over the years, "So you quit your job as an engineer? Did you experience some sort of trauma or witness something that triggered all of this?"

"Nope."

There was no shocking moment of truth. There was no

dramatic scene in a developing country that opened my eyes to what I previously was unaware.

It was very ordinary. Boring might be the best way to describe it. And my realization didn't come to me in an instant. Rather it crept up on me over a period of time as I grew to gradually realize the truth that was in front of me all the time. It was as plain as the nose on my face. I realized I was fortunate and my life was a gift. All aspects of it, the good, the bad, and the ugly. While I consider the world a playground, don't extrapolate from my mindset that I have a life free from stress, hurt, anger, loss, suffering and pain. I've got all of these, but I refuse to let them define me.

GET STARTED NOW

Being hard-wired one way or the other doesn't need to determine your mindset. You have a choice. You can wait to see your life as a gift, which means waiting to have a thriving mindset. It is your choice. But I would ask, if you want a thriving mindset, why wait one more year before acknowledging your life is a gift? Or why wait until you experience a life-altering event? Why not acknowledge it today? By starting today, you get to spend more time thriving now and you'll be better prepared when the inevitable challenges come your way. Nothing happens overnight, so be patient, but begin today.

We have a whole chapter on the simple habits to build a thriving mindset, but we want to get you started on exercising your gratitude muscles right now. The simplest and most effective next step is to make a commitment to make a gratitude list every day, and list three things. This is the aerobic gratitude workout. It rewires your brain by forcing you to look for the good. It reorients you to thriving because you're focused on the good in your life.

We want this to become a habit. It is my deepest desire that you will do this one simple habit every day for the rest of your life. I haven't missed a day in more than ten years now, and it's been a game changer for me; I know it will be for you, too. You will have easy days, and there will be days it will feel impossible to make a list. You will feel that it is really working some days, and other days you'll wonder why you're doing it and think it's a waste of time. Persevere. Stick it out. Carry on. Keep making your gratitude list. Here are a few tips to get started.

Pick your format—electronic, app, journal, or notepad. Don't just list them in your head. Write or type them. It takes a little extra effort, but helps the rewiring process in your brain.

Find a time that works for you—first thing in the morning, before you go to bed, when you arrive at the office, when you're waiting for the kids, before dinner, whenever. There is no magic, just find a time that works for you and try to stick to that time so it becomes part of your routine.

Use a reminder—if you're writing electronically, you could set up an automated notification. If you're using a journal, you could place it on your bedside table or on your desk at the office or somewhere highly visible so that you'll see it.

It doesn't matter how we're wired. We can change, even if we think that gratitude is not for us. This was reinforced one afternoon at the gym when a young man approached me and said, "I don't know if you remember me, but I was in one of your gratitude sessions a few years ago. At the time, gratitude really wasn't my thing. I liked your enthusiasm and passion for the topic, but the only reason I was there was because my employer made me take the training. No offense, it's just not who I am."

He had my attention. I thought, "Where is he going with this?"

He continued, "Then, about a year later, I ran into some very challenging times in my life, and I didn't know how I was going to cope. Then I remembered that gratitude journal you gave me. I thought to myself, 'What have I got to lose?' So I gave it a try and within a few weeks I couldn't believe the difference it made in my life. I truly believe it helped me make it through one of the most challenging times in my adult life."

"Whew! What a relief." —me thinking again.

Then he said, "I still use the journal, but not every day, and I just want to thank you for sharing it with me."

"You're welcome." I said. "Keep up the journal and don't beat yourself up if you miss a day here and there. Thanks for letting me know."

In the next chapter, we'll flip one of the reasons why people don't practice gratitude into one of the fundamental reasons why they should. And as for the guy at the gym, I didn't remember his name, but I recognized his face. I am grateful that he shared his experience, because it reveals the Fourth Law of Grateful Leadership.

FOURTH LAW OF GRATEFUL LEADERSHIP

GRATITUDE IS FOR EVERYONE, INCLUDING YOU

IMPLICATIONS FOR YOU:

You can change, and those you lead can change. Some people will resist change and will need your encouragement to change. This is a cornerstone of great leadership: influencing others to achieve what they cannot currently believe they can accomplish.

Be patient with yourself and with others, because it takes time to change. Change doesn't happen overnight, and rarely do others change at the pace you might want them to.

ASK YOURSELF THE FOLLOWING QUESTIONS:

What beliefs do I have about myself that might be preventing me from building a more thriving mindset?

What privilege do I have?

What is the best way for me to make a list of three things I'm grateful for?

Am I willing to commit to making my gratitude list for the next 30 days?

KNOWING WHAT I KNOW, WHAT DO I TAKE AWAY FROM THIS CHAPTER?

CHAPTER 5

IT'S TOO SIMPLE

THERE ARE THREE THINGS I discovered about simple solutions. They can be:
- hard to spot
- hard to implement
- very effective

SIMPLE IS HARD TO SPOT

A friend of mine has a guy in his neighbourhood who rummages through the garbage collecting bottles to return for refunds. One day he saw him in his backyard rooting through a special bag he'd been saving. He ran out of the house. "Hey, if they're at the curb you can have them. But these ones out back are for my son's hockey team."

The guy said, "Oh, I'm sorry. I didn't know. And it's ok, because I'm having a pretty good month. So far I've donated almost $200 to the shelter."

My friend was gobsmacked. "You mean you donate the

money from these bottles to the homeless shelter?"

The guy said, "Yeah, I got pretty much everything I need."

My friend was surprised and taken aback. It stayed on his mind for a few weeks. Then, while he was up on a ladder working on his house, he heard an unusual noise that echoed throughout the neighbourhood. And sure enough, it was the guy. He had a grocery buggy full of bottles that rattled as it bounced down the uneven sidewalk. As he looked down from the ladder, the next thing he saw was the guy heading to the backyard. My friend couldn't believe it. "Hey," he yelled, "Remember, out back is for my son."

The guy looked up and very calmly said, "Yeah, I know. You told me a couple weeks ago. I just had some extra bottles and thought your son could use them."

He was speechless.

I would have done the same thing if I were in my friend's shoes. And because of that, I would have missed something very, very simple—a simple act of kindness and generosity. Nothing extraordinary. Just simple. And I would have missed it because it was so simple.

Simple things, like the importance of the practice of gratitude, can be hard to spot.

SIMPLE IS NOT EASY

Mom and Dad were smokers. They each smoked two to three packs of cigarettes a day. As a youth, I hated to see my parents smoke and at times the five kids would gang up on them to get them to quit. We were afraid for them. We knew it wasn't healthy and it was harming them. We knew they wanted to quit, in spite of Mom, who would often say,

"I love my cigarettes." When I was in my early 20's both of them eventually quit. First, Dad quit and about four years later Mom kicked the habit. Having my parents quit smoking was such a relief to me. I remember, just after Dad quit smoking, I started having a dream that I described as a recurring nightmare. I dreamt that Dad started smoking again. I'd wake up wondering if it really happened or not, and fortunately it was always just a dream. These dreams went on for about five years.

Here's the thing: quitting smoking is simple but it's not easy.

The same holds true for gratitude. Yes, gratitude is very very simple. But it is far from easy. The demands of life, urgent priorities, the ongoing series of challenges that are part of the human condition and everyday living distract us and can make this simple idea difficult. Whether it's caring for aging parents, concern for a sick relative, worry about children making the right decisions, pressures at work, or stress about financial security. There are no shortage of life circumstances that make finding the good in a situation difficult. And of course, let's not forget the unrelenting force that is constantly pulling us down into survival mindset.

SIMPLE IS EFFECTIVE

I was a participant in a leadership session that a colleague, Kevin, was leading. He was talking about recognition and how powerful it is (recognition is a form of gratitude expression). Kevin asked the audience, "Raise your hand if you've ever received a thank you note or card from your supervisor or boss's boss." Together with most other people in the room, I raised my hand. He asked, "How long ago was that?"

Answers ranged from six months to 25 years. Then Kevin asked a very powerful question. "If you still have that thank you card, raise your hand." Again, most people lifted their hands as the lights went on in our minds about the powerful, simple gesture of writing a thank you card. He jokingly asked how many people still have their latest anniversary card. Few people raised their hands, but most of us laughed. I was one of the ones who had kept the thank you cards, and still have one that I've been hanging onto for more than 26 years now. I was also one of the ones who didn't have my latest anniversary card. I was filled with mixed emotions: guilt for not keeping a card given to me by the most important person in my world, and empowerment for finding evidence of the power of a simple thank you.

Simple works. Don't fall for the fallacy that complex problems need complex solutions. Being endlessly stuck in survival mindset is a complex problem but it does not require a complex solution. There is a simple solution to breaking through to living a thriving life and being a Thriving Leader. There is a natural attractiveness to a fancy, complex solution, because "complex" often implies a high level of sophistication, credibility and confidence in solving the problem at hand. Sending a space shuttle into orbit multiple times is complex and requires a complex solution. Yet rocket scientists are discovering simpler solutions are possible. These simpler solutions cost less and require less turnaround time between launches, two important considerations for reusable spacecraft.

SIMPLE IN THE MOST ORDINARY OF TIMES

The simplicity of gratitude and its power is often realized at the simplest of times. For example, when I call Dad and the call goes to voicemail, I get to hear my mom's voice. It's been more than five years since she died, and Dad hasn't changed the outgoing message. It's still Mom. There are times I call it when I know Dad is not home just so I can hear Mom's voice. When Mom set up the voicemail years and years ago, she had no idea what a gift it would be to us, nor how impactful it would be. The notion that there's incredible power in simplicity is something that, deep down, we know it to be true. For example, this truth is revealed to you: When a small child hugs you. When you witness a beautiful sunset. When your supervisor goes out of her way to ask you about something that is meaningful to you. When a friend takes the time to listen. When someone you haven't seen in a long time shows up at a family funeral. When your teenage or young adult children ask you for advice. And interestingly, what do these cost? Nothing.

You may be thinking, "This is common sense. This is nothing more than motherhood." If so, you are correct. Yet, these simple, grace-filled moments are powerful recalibrators. They recalibrate us by reminding us of what we know to be true, making us less likely to take our lives and the people in them for granted.

"Simplicity is the ultimate sophistication."

—Leonardo da Vinci

GENUINENESS IS KEY

When we talk about gratitude, there are two facets of being genuine. The first is in accepting or receiving with genuineness. The second is expressing our gratitude genuinely.

Let's look first at receiving. For the four boys growing up, Christmas gifts from Nanny were seldom a surprise. Once the first sweater or jacket was opened we all knew what we were getting. I'm sure Mom had a lot of say in helping Nanny pick out our gifts, as Mom tried to outfit four growing boys who were hard on clothes. I can't speak for my brothers, but I know I wasn't the most grateful child when the gift was a sweater or a jacket, or anything that wasn't a toy. Mom and Dad tried to teach us to be thankful and appreciate any gift we received. At a young age I just wasn't able to connect the dots in order to be genuinely grateful. Today, however, it's different. When I receive a gift, even a gift that say I don't want or don't like, I'm able to be grateful for the gift. The gift is a symbol of someone's thoughtfulness and love. It is not meant to replace their care and love. For example, I received a shirt that didn't fit me comfortably and it was clearly not my taste in style, yet I was grateful for:

1. The fact the giver thought of me,
2. The time and energy they sacrificed to find the shirt, wrap it and include a card, and
3. That they cared enough to give me a gift.

These positive thoughts were not manufactured nor recited by rote; they were genuine. When my mind is filled with gratitudes like these, it makes me feel totally different than if I had thought, "This shirt doesn't fit and I would never wear it; even if it fit, as it looks like it's something for an old man." The grateful thoughts support a thriving mindset and help me feel better about myself and the person who gave me the gift, leading to a sense of abundance, which allows me to be a Thriving Leader. The negative thoughts fill me with entitlement, focusing on what I don't have, leaving me with the feeling of scarcity and a survival mindset. What is critical though, is that my gratitude must be genuine.

Let's look at expressing gratitude. Expressing gratitude genuinely will almost happen automatically if you've taken the time to consider what you're grateful for about a situation. Being genuine in expressing gratitude requires one thing and one thing only—that you truly and genuinely recognize what you've received. If you turn your mind to what you'll get in return for expressing your gratitude, you run the risk of not being genuine which, as you know, will backfire on you.

The last vehicle we purchased was accompanied by a couple serious mix ups by the dealership which cost us a significant amount of time and anxiety. We purchased it out of province, and we were not pleased with the customer service we received during the sale, nor in the follow-up in trying to resolve the issue. The situation escalated to the general manager who seemed extremely empathetic and genuine in his concern for the troubles they caused us, troubles that were easily avoidable. The general manager offered us some compensation by upgrading, at no cost to us, several interior trim options on the vehicle. It seemed like he listened to our concerns and understood our frustrations, and we felt that his offer was fair and reasonable, so I sent him an email agreeing to the proposed upgrades. That evening I received an email from him. Here it is word for word other than that I changed the brand name to "the manufacturer":

> "All I would ask in return is that you help me out
> in the two surveys that you will soon be receiving
> from the manufacturer. I would never ask anybody
> to lie or state any untruths on the survey, but if you

did not return it to the manufacturer, I would be appreciative. They have recently gone to an all or nothing scoring system where if we do not receive the absolute highest marks in all categories, they score the survey as a 0. I kind of understand what they are trying to do, meaning if the customer isn't completely satisfied, then we have failed. It would take us months to recover from two bad surveys. If this makes sense to you, please e-mail me back or give me a call later today if you would like to discuss it."

We declined his offer. His offer and thankfulness were not genuine. They were given so he could get something back in exchange. Although we had previously felt that he had listened to our concerns and understood our frustrations, we walked away feeling used and unappreciated. The last time we visited the city where we bought the car we discovered the dealership no longer exists.

AN EMBARRASSING HARD-TO-SPOT EXPERIENCE

I shudder to think back on how I repeatedly, and completely, missed a golden rule of gratitude. The following personal story unfolded countless times in our marriage and occasionally resurfaces when I lose sight of reality and fall into survival mode. For years I would nag my wife Lyn as we headed to a friend's place for dinner. "Why do we have to bring a bottle of wine? They have lots of wine. It's not like they need it." Sometimes it was wine, sometimes it was flowers, sometimes it was a package of funny napkins and a candle. Regardless, my response was virtually the same every time.

"What are we bringing that for? They are hosting us!" I can't say I remember how Lyn responded each time, but it must have been very frustrating for her, because I did it without fail. Then one day while reading *The Several Spiritual Laws of Success* by Deepak Chopra, the answer to my questioning was revealed. Lyn was sitting next to me when I read a chapter on bringing a gift when you're invited into someone's home. The gift was meant in thanksgiving to their hospitality. And it needn't cost anything. The gift could be a prayer, a handmade carving, a bottle of wine or anything. It was in that moment I realized that you don't bring a bottle of wine because Chris and Kelliann or Dave and Michelle need another bottle of wine, you bring it because you're grateful, genuinely grateful, for their gift of hospitality. Wow. It's obvious today, and what a feeling of peace and joy it brought and continues to bring me. This simple perspective shift adjusted my filter from surviving mode to thriving mode and reoriented me toward a thriving mindset. Looking back, it amazes me how I couldn't see this overly simple mindset mistake.

Herein lies the special magic of gratitude: It is in the genuine receiving and giving of gratitude that we create an upward virtuous cycle of positive influence. This is foundational to Thriving Leadership, whether you're thanking someone for a job well done, appreciating a volunteer for their hard work or congratulating a spouse for tidying up the house while you were out for the night.

When you receive gratitude, be genuine, and when you give gratitude, be genuine. Genuineness is always obvious in the fullness of time. You will know if you're genuine; others will, too. And how will you know? As a mentor shared with me when I asked him, "How will I know if I'm fooling myself, Joe?" He said, "You'll know."

GRATITUDE IS NOT A QUICK FIX

Don't expect overnight results from yourself or from your team. Building a grateful frame of mind is a simple and effective way to reorient yourself to a thriving mindset. Commit to taking action every day to build your gratitude muscles, and they will serve you well throughout your life. Be disciplined to put in the work to develop and strengthen the four habits we cover later in the book. For now, stick to your gratitude list and keep writing it each day. This habit is foundational, and if you've already started it, you should notice a difference in how you feel, even if only temporarily. Building a robust, thriving mindset takes time. In fact, it takes a lifetime, so be patient, both with yourself and with those you lead.

Although gratitude has transformed my life, I don't for a minute think that just because it is the best predictor of human flourishing that it is the one and only personal growth solution I should implement to ensure I become a Thriving Leader. Therefore, I exercise, eat healthy, pray, socialize and attend to my personal development through reading, seminars, and coaching. Interestingly, as the research has found, gratitude helps me with these other personal growth activities.

In keeping with the theme of simplicity, let's not over-complicate your take-away from this chapter. Keep up with the one simple practice we introduced in Chapter 4—make a list of what you're grateful for. Do this daily. Shoot for three items on your list. We'll dig into this deeper in later chapters, but this simple practice is the foundation for thriving leadership and ultimately for a thriving life. There are days when you will experience challenges which will make it seem difficult or impossible to identify just one thing you're grateful for. But don't let your guard down. Hold onto the belief that you are worthy and have lots to be grateful for. There is good in the situation. It will be your job to find it. If you're not making a gratitude list daily, make the commitment to do so. If you've been listing your gratitudes daily, congratulations! Keep it up. If there's something you want to list again and again (like your freedom), that's great, but consider looking deeper into that gratitude. Be more specific about the benefits you've received or identify the people who made it happen (as best you can name them) and what they did.

This chapter has focused on the simplicity of gratitude and how its simplicity can be a barrier for many people to see and accept gratitude as a legitimate means to leading a thriving life. In the next chapter, we'll cover why gratitude is anything but a Pollyanna take on the world. Take comfort in the Fifth Law of Grateful Leadership which requires no super powers whatsoever. It reinforces the need for ordinary everyday actions.

FIFTH LAW OF GRATEFUL LEADERSHIP

Keep it simple

Implications for you:

Simple means simple. It doesn't mean easy, though. Losing weight is simple, but it's not easy. Quitting smoking is simple, but not easy. We don't want to overstate the magnitude of the gratitude journey before you, but it will not be easy. Your success in being a grateful, thriving leader is predicated on:

1. Being consistent (for now keep your focus on the gratitude list; there are more habits coming later) and
2. Being genuine in your gratitude. And remember to be a grateful, thriving leader, you don't have to spend a dime.

ASK YOURSELF THE FOLLOWING QUESTIONS:

What simple things do I wish I had learned sooner?

When am I most genuine, and how can I be like that more often?

Am I willing to put in the effort to strengthen my gratitude practice?

KNOWING WHAT I KNOW, WHAT DO I TAKE AWAY FROM THIS CHAPTER?

CHAPTER 6

IT'S NOT POLLYANNA

OUR SON NICK HAD a full hip replacement four days after his 28th birthday. We are uncertain the cause, because he had no serious accidents nor sports injuries growing up. One hip, the bad one, was bone-on-bone, but his other hip was perfectly fine. No sign of arthritis. It's something of a mystery, really. A hip replacement for young people is unusual, but it's not un-heard of, as the nurses said they usually see about one patient per month like Nick. As parents, it was upsetting to learn that one of our kids required a procedure of this magnitude. There was the heartache we felt because of the pain he had been living through, and the impact the surgery would have on his life during recovery. This was magnified by the un-certainty it held for his future, knowing this wouldn't be his last hip surgery, either. There was the anxiousness as we ap-proached the surgery date: "What if something goes wrong during surgery?" All of this thinking was survival thinking, and it is quite natural; however, it did not need to define how we dealt with the situation.

I was committed to finding the good in the situation without being Pollyannaish. I asked, "What's good about the fact that Nick needs a hip replacement at age 28?" I surprised myself with how quickly the list began to grow.

- Nick would longer be in pain
- He had a top notch surgeon who had successfully completed this operation thousands of times
- Our healthcare system took care of the expenses, so it wouldn't encumber him with any financial burden
- Nick was in good physical shape, so his recovery would go quickly and he'd be back to normal life in no time
- He was able to get the surgery scheduled quickly and conveniently between his school terms so it had little impact on his education
- While it is unlikely the new hip will last him the rest of his life, technology is making replacement hips last longer and longer so he may only need one more
- Nick had a very positive approach to dealing with this
- His wife Kelsey was there to care for him and help him through his recuperation
- He was able to borrow a walker and a few assistive aids so, again, there was no cost to him

This list of "good" was reassuring to me as a father. The fact that I could see so much good in this situation didn't mean that I didn't care or that I wasn't compassionate about the pain and suffering he experienced or would have to deal with through his recovery. It was quite comforting because, like any human, in the lead up to the surgery, I could feel the unrelenting force at work. "What if something bad happens during surgery?" "What if he doesn't wake up?" Pragmatically, I have little control over either of these nagging concerns, but I would go back to my list of good and realize that my survival mindset was trying to mislead me. "Look, we've got a very talented surgeon who does this surgery almost every day—a couple times each day—and he does it very successfully!" My ability to see the good in the situation allowed me to turn to logical evidence, which helped me deal with the crappier aspects of his circumstances. It returned a sense of control to my world for something that I had absolutely no control over. More importantly, being able to see the good in this very serious situation prevented anxiety, fear and a survival mindset from spilling over into the other areas of my life.

It's worth mentioning briefly that I always try to avoid comparison when I look for good. For example, I could have included in the list, "At least he wasn't diagnosed with cancer." While this is true, comparing takes my mindset down a level or two by focusing on what others have or don't have instead of focusing on what I have. The tendency to compare is a detriment to a thriving mindset and is really important, so we'll leave it to discuss in greater depth in Chapter 7.

As a father, I'm very proud of Nick, who modeled a positive attitude from the day he was diagnosed, a mindset that has continued throughout his recovery, which is ongoing as I write this book.

A grateful mindset is not an ignorant approach to dealing with Nick's surgery, nor in any aspect of life. We know gratitude orients us toward a thriving mindset. But there's still the cynic in us that thinks gratitude is akin to an ostrich sticking its head in the sand in an attempt to make a bad circumstance disappear. Nothing could be further from the truth when it comes to gratitude. Gratitude does not allow us to ignore the crap in our lives nor does it make the crap go away. But gratitude enables us to reframe how we make sense of a situation, which in turn better equips us to deal with whatever circumstances we face. Nancy, a colleague and mentor of mine who is a trusted advisor to my country's top CEOs and business owners, says, "Never make an important decision in a negative state of mind." Why? Because when you're in a negative frame of mind, you're in survival mode because the executive function of your brain is compromised and you're less likely to rely on higher order cognitive processes like generative thinking and self-awareness.

WHAT IS YOUR WORLDVIEW?

Gratitude emerges from one's perspective. We all have perspectives and we each have a dominant worldview that is shaped by our life circumstances, values and beliefs. It is through our perspective and worldview that we make sense of the events and situations that come into our lives. When our perspective is one biased toward noticing the good in a situation, we are more likely to experience gratitude. People who have a greater disposition toward being grateful are more likely to have a perspective that is attuned to the good. This very much is supported in The Cycle of Leadership Influence model presented in Chapter 3.

ENGAGEMENT, MINDSET AND GRATITUDE

After more than a decade working with companies to help them bring more gratitude to work each day, I regularly have discussions about employee engagement. In a nutshell, employee engagement is a measure of an employee's emotional commitment to their work and their employer. At first, I didn't see the immediate connection between gratitude and engagement. I continued to be surprised by the fact that, in the 15+ years since the concept of employee engagement has gained widespread attention and Gallup has been measuring it globally, there has been virtually no change in employee engagement. None! Bottom line is that only 30% of the workforce is engaged and emotionally committed at work. Based on data I've seen, it is estimated this lack of engagement is costing employers more than $2,600 per employee every single year.

As I dug deeper, I found that feeling appreciated is a key component to the ultimate goal of employee engagement, which provides the direct connection to gratitude at work—a connection I had been seeking. For many years, I knew it was there, but wasn't able to make sense of the complex geometry of relationships, emotion, and results. The most recent research on gratitude at work confirms that 80% of people would work harder for a more grateful boss (aka—a Thriving Leader), but sadly reports that only 10% of people express gratitude at work on a daily basis. Furthermore, 60% of people express gratitude at work on an annual basis either two times, once or never. That's right, two or fewer times per year.

The nagging feelings left from the many conversations I had with business owners and CEOs in the shadow of a rapidly growing management consulting industry focused on employee engagement ultimately led me to develop a framework. It connects gratitude to the end goal of increasing employee engagement and building a thriving culture. While the language used in this framework is geared around a workplace, it extends to volunteer groups, sports teams and families—anywhere we have groups of people interacting together. The framework is illustrated below and the definitions that follow should make the framework self-explanatory:

The bottom row illustrates the three possible states of gratitude you can be in at any given time. Regardless, you are in one of these states.

ENTITLEMENT	COMPLACENCY	THRIVING
ACTIVELY DISENGAGED	NOT ENGAGED	ENGAGED
INGRATEFUL	UNGRATEFUL	GRATEFUL

INGRATEFUL
Feeling resentful for your situation. Feeling that you deserve more. Feeling that what you have isn't good enough or that whoever provided you a benefit has an ulterior selfish motive.

UNGRATEFUL
There's no feeling at all, because this is the absence of gratitude. Neither grateful nor ingrateful. It's a state of being

unaware, similar to when you take something for granted.

GRATEFUL
A positive feeling of appreciation that recognizes what others have done for you, accompanied by a genuine desire to say thank you; usually recognizing the benefits received and the sacrifices made by others.

"Ingratitude is an abomination."—*Seneca*

The middle row illustrates the three categories that Gallup and similar organizations use to characterize the level of employee engagement. Open your mind to interpret the definitions more broadly as people engagement, which essentially boils down to emotional commitment.

ACTIVELY DISENGAGED
Disgruntled. They would go out of their way to hinder the organization. They try to persuade others to join their ranks.

NOT ENGAGED
They are present but really aren't present. They could readily become either Engaged or Actively Disengaged.

ENGAGED
They are emotionally committed to their work. They love what they do and are active supporters at work, even for difficult things like change.

The top row illustrates three mindsets that come from our beliefs, attitudes, and how we think of our lives and the situations and stories that define us as individuals.

ENTITLEMENT
I deserve more and others should step up and do something about it.

COMPLACENCY
It's fine as-is. I don't really care and don't think about it.

THRIVING
I want to make it the best it can be.

As you can see, gratitude is the absence of complacency and entitlement.

Can you see how ingrateful, actively disengaged and entitlement are similar? The same holds for ungrateful, not engaged and complacent. And lastly, we have the mark of a Thriving Leader—grateful, engaged and thriving. Thriving Leaders live a life rooted in gratitude, continuously develop a growth mindset that moves upward and are emotionally committed to whatever they set their hand to. Thriving Leadership applies at the executive table, in service clubs, in community libraries, on family vacations and in small work teams.

Being actively disengaged, ingrateful and entitled at work might look like holding back, not giving your best, and ruminating over the fact you think you deserve a position that was given to someone else. In a service club, it could be refusing to help on an important project because the project was not fully funded the way you had envisioned. It might be taking credit for someone else's work. It's quite easy to spot this behaviour and usually other people are the first to notice ingrateful behaviour. It is survival behaviour at its finest.

Complacent, not engaged, ungrateful behaviour can be hard to spot. It's like being on cruise control and not paying attention. Others may see it but they may just as easily not notice it. It might look like waiting to take action on something that obviously needs attention. It might be failing to recognize someone for their contribution to a project, whether the project is a complex strategy report, emptying the dishwasher, or leading a group of volunteers to clean up a community park. While it might be a stretch to describe these as surviving behaviours, they are anything but thriving behaviours. In my opinion and based on my life experience, complacent behaviours will eventually change into surviving behaviours or thriving behaviours. The unrelenting force will bring on the survival mindset unless individual initiative helps rise to a thriving mindset.

Engaged, growth-minded, grateful behaviour defines Thriving Leadership. While these behaviours are obvious, they can be hard to notice because our brains are wired to be hypersensitive to negative experiences and negative behaviours. Thriving Leaders do things like publicly acknowledge the contributions of other people, go out of their way to help someone (even when they won't receive any credit), take time to learn from their mistakes and apologize without making excuses.

When you look at the political environment, what is the characteristic behaviour most apparent to you? Is political leadership surviving or thriving? While this applies to leaders in all walks of life, if we desire the type of world we want our grandchildren to grow up in, I believe we need our political leaders to spend more time thriving and much less time surviving.

PERSPECTIVE IS WHAT MATTERS

There is power in perspective. When you sit three rows from

the ice surface at a hockey game you can hear the players breathe and speak with each other and you can almost feel impact of every hit. You have a close up view. If, at the same game, you sit three rows down from the top of the arena, you can see the play develop and the strategy each team is using, whether on offense or defense. You have a macro view of the entire game. In this example, both people are watching the same game but have very different perspectives which influence how they think and feel about the game. The viewer from the top can't hear the players breathe. Those who sit rinkside can't see the larger picture of the game.

Gratitude works similarly. With a grateful perspective you are able to see the good in any situation, a view that is otherwise invisible from a negative perspective. This grateful perspective begins by holding to the belief, "I am worthy and have much to be grateful for." This opens us to the possibility that good exists and gets us looking for the good, no matter the circumstance.

When You See the Good

When your mindset is thriving your perspective filter is set to see the good which triggers an addictive, calming feeling that culminates from the production of the dopamine, serotonin and oxytocin elixir that your brain dumps into your system. Probably the cheapest feel-good drugs you'll ever get to use.

The thriving mindset essentially tames the reptilian brain, which is geared toward survival. Switching your perspective filter from negative (surviving) to positive (thriving) moves you from scarcity (where there's never enough) to abundance (where there is always plenty). The thriving mindset is free from the long-term presence of survival mindset chemicals like adrenaline and cortisol which are associated with freeze, flight or fight. The thriving, grateful mindset transforms fear to flourishing which carries into daily living in all aspects of your life.

Fear and scarcity drive avoidance behaviours, and are rooted in the motivation to survive. Avoidance behaviours include retreat, escape, delay, distance and protect. On the other hand, abundance and gratitude are associated with approach behaviours which include being curious, adventurous, and innovative, and demonstrating initiative.

Avoidance behaviours help us survive, while approach behaviours helps us thrive. In my opinion, in 2019 and beyond, we need to spend more time thriving and less time, much less time, surviving. These approach behaviours come more naturally the more we develop a thriving mindset.

The gratitude that results from seeing good also helps us develop stronger interpersonal relationships, because gratitude makes us more "other focused" and less "self focused." This shift in focus, which happens naturally (and very gradually) as we age, is a result of us simply noticing more about what others are doing in our lives. The "other focused" bias helps counteract the unrelenting force that is pulling you downward toward survival and strengthens your ability to notice the good around you, so you can spend more time thriving.

The argument that gratitude is nothing more than a Pollyanna attitude is fueled by the human tendency to assign more weight to negative circumstances than positive ones. As a thriving leader you must understand that for most people, this tendency is unconsciously accepted as fact. Therefore, an important part of your leadership role is to persevere in helping everyone understand the truth about having a positive, grateful perspective.

PRONOIA
I discovered this idea from Dr. Robert Emmons, the world's leading scientific expert on gratitude.

Here's the gist of it: Pronoia is a condition wherein the perspective filter to your brain operates on the premise that everyone around you is conspiring in your favour. The opposite condition, paranoia is a household word; no surprise, there's the unrelenting force again. Paranoia is when we think everyone around us is conspiring against us. Pronoia is the antithesis of paranoia. When was the last time you felt the world was conspiring in your favour? Were you on a team? Was it as a young child when the world truly is a playground?

I encourage you to develop a strong sense of pronoia.

Finding good in the ups and downs of business

In the first year running my business, I earned 25% of the income from my previous job and virtually the entire amount went to paying expenses for getting started: marketing materials, travel, a computer, some basic office supplies and furniture.

This provided the ideal opportunity to test my mettle in my newfound role as a gratitude practitioner. It could have been so easy to get caught up in the stress and anxiety of a significant drop in household income. But I didn't. Lyn was concerned, though. I remember her asking me in that first year, "How much longer are we going to try this?"

I thought to myself, "Try this? Baby, this is what I do now!" Even though I wasn't doing much of it, at least not getting paid for what I was doing.

Through that first year, I focused on the good and what I was grateful for. I had already been practicing gratitude for a few years, so maintaining a thriving mindset was getting easier. In that first year, I had so much to be grateful for, and I knew it. I was grateful for my wife, Lyn, who buoyed me with much needed encouragement and single-handedly supported our family financially. I was grateful for those first few clients who took a risk on hiring me, and grateful for the referrals they provided. I was grateful for my very first client, who paid 10% more than we agreed because he felt he got more value. I was grateful to be able to work from my home office and save more than an hour most days by not having to commute. I was grateful to have more time around the kids who were in their late teens. I was grateful for the way the kids poked fun at me using air quotes when they talked about me "working." I was grateful for all this and more.

Fortunately, the next year I matched the income from my previous employment. As the business evolved over the next 12 years, there were a couple very slow years. Some of it was due to the economy and some of it was due to shifting and repositioning the business. It was incredibly difficult during one of the repositioning phases in 2014, because at a time when revenue was down, we were also reinvesting a lot back into the business, and I was heavily committed as the Chair of a university volunteer board. Our personal debt grew at that time as a result. While this bothered me because I don't like using a line of credit to pay for groceries, I knew it was temporary. At the time I was grateful that we had a line of credit we could use. I was grateful for Lyn who again shouldered the financial support for our family. I was grateful for supportive friends like Derek and Allan who I could talk to. I was grateful to Cathy, who invited me to teach at a local University years earlier, and for the part-time teaching income that was much needed that year. I was grateful for all I was learning on the volunteer boards and the support and time invested by my board colleagues. I was grateful to Neil and his brilliant marketing mind as he helped me navigate the rebranding of the business. I was grateful for the feeling of excitement and anticipation for the future in spite of the fact there was no guarantee.

I would have rather not gone through the rough years in

the business; however, I know, and truly believe, that being able to see the good and be grateful is what helped me that year spend more time thriving and less time surviving. The thriving mindset equipped me to better deal with the challenges and ultimately overcome them. The thriving mindset was the direct result of a well-established and regular gratitude practice.

Keep up the habit of making a list of what you're grateful for. In particular when you encounter a situation or circumstance in your life that is particularly challenging, focus on that situation and identify three things you're grateful for about that particular challenge.

SIXTH LAW OF GRATEFUL LEADERSHIP

THERE IS GOOD IN VIRTUALLY EVERY SITUATION

IMPLICATIONS FOR YOU:
It's easy to find and ruminate over all the negative in your life, however, if you give yourself the permission to find the good in your circumstances, it will transform your mindset from surviving to thriving.

Gratitude transforms life from a series of positive and negative events into an ever-present realization of goodness and growth.

ASK YOURSELF THE FOLLOWING QUESTIONS:

How would I describe or characterize my worldview?

How do I rate myself on the scale of entitlement, complacency and thriving? Am I engaged in all that I set my mind to?

When am I most susceptible to focusing on the negative in a situation? What can I do about that tendency?

What do I think about the idea of pronoia? Where do I see it in my life?

In what life circumstance have I had difficulty finding the good? What good can I see in that circumstance now? What am I grateful for about it?

KNOWING WHAT I KNOW, WHAT DO I TAKE AWAY FROM THIS CHAPTER?

CHAPTER 7

THE UNRELENTING FORCE

I AM A FAST eater. For the life of me, I had no idea I ate fast, and was caught off guard when Lyn mentioned it to me very early in our relationship, long before we were married. We were out for dinner at a restaurant. I was trying to impress her by being on my best behaviour. I was using all my table manners and sitting with great posture. By the time I was halfway through my meal, Lyn looked up at me in puzzlement and said, "How is your meal?"

I said, "Good. How's yours?"

She said, "Good. But how did you know yours was good?"

"What do you mean?" I said.

She said, "You ate that so fast, I don't know how you could have tasted anything."

She was right, I was fast. So in that restaurant, at that exact moment, I consciously decided to slow down while eating. I'd chew deliberately and make sure I chewed each bite 20 or 30 times before swallowing. Between mouthfuls, I'd lay down my knife and fork. All this slowed me down, and it worked for a bite or two, but then, without even realizing it,

I'd be right back to my fast eating again—like an alligator on the riverbank thrashing my freshly-caught prey.

Mom and Dad didn't teach us to eat our meals fast, but the best I figure is that it was a habit that developed at our dining room table. With five kids, if you wanted a second helping, you didn't want to be the last to finish your first serving. And as kids, we were all pretty fast eaters, so I guess we developed the habit so that we would get what we wanted before it was all gone.

I've seen this tendency in other large families, but not in all large families. The only person I know who consistently eats faster than me is one of my best friends, Derek. He doesn't look like he eats fast and neither do I. But he comes from a family of 10, so I suspect similar sibling rules applied in his household.

There's no question that this habit of eating fast was developed and motivated out of fear of not having enough food and the ultimate need to survive. Habits are powerful, in particular survival habits. Occasionally, I will try to eat a meal slowly, but it ends up like that first time Lyn and I ate, where she called me out on it: I'm back to eating fast without even realizing it. Here I am, at age 55, and I'm catapulted into survival mode every time I sit down at the dinner table.

Our brains have evolved significantly over the course of human history, however, the reptilian part of our brain, which is geared toward survival, has a disproportionate amount of control over how we feel, think and act. It influences more than how we show up at the dinner table; ultimately, it influences how we show up as leaders in our lives.

THE DICHOTOMY:
SURVIVING VS. THRIVING

There is an endless line of people who want to thrive (I would argue all of humanity wants to thrive). Yet I see and hear from far too many people who feel stuck surviving and struggling in an endless cycle of never having enough to be happy. In Chapters 2 and 3, we discussed the unrelenting force that is constantly trying to rob you of a thriving life as it pushes you downward to survival mode; in fact, that ancient part of your brain would like you to think you need to operate in a prehistoric evolutionary state of survival.

The unrelenting force is constant like gravity. When you're thriving, the unrelenting force is at work pulling you down to a survival mindset. If you're surviving, the unrelenting force already has a strong grip on you, which makes it difficult to get unstuck from the survival mindset. The unrelenting force catastrophizes even the smallest of daily challenges. It tries to persuade your brain that there is a pervasive and constant stream of evidence that justifies the need to react with a survival mindset. There is an endless list of everyday challenges that the unrelenting force will magnify to tempt you to react. This includes irritants like getting cut-off in traffic, spilling your morning coffee, having a key employee calling in sick again, getting in an argument with someone you love, having your ideas rejected, and the list goes on and on.

OUR BRAINS DON'T ALWAYS HELP US

OUR BRAINS ACCENTUATE THE NEGATIVE:

Our brain's ability to notice the negative is credited as one of the big reasons humans exist today. Our ancestors were able to survive in treacherous conditions in the face of much larger and faster predators. This tendency is still hardwired into the human brain today, and makes us pay more attention to negative events than positive events and circumstances. Think back to a performance review at work, a graded exam or paper at school, or feedback on a new skill you're learning. If you're like most people, most of your mental energy is focused on the 5-10% of constructive criticism as opposed to the 90-95% of praise and support. My colleague Nancy lives by the adage, "Feedback is a gift." It can quickly drag you down into a negative spiral, but she reframes it into learning that will make her a better person. She is grateful for feedback. Our hypersensitivity to negative stimulus drags us down into survival mode.

OUR BRAINS ADAPT:

When good things happen in our lives (get a raise, buy a new car, start a new relationship, receive a positive medical diagnosis), we initially notice the good, but quickly start to adapt to these good fortunes. This causes that initial feeling of joy and happiness to fade over time and often it completely disappears. Adaptation happens slowly without us even noticing, and before we know it, we're back to survival mode, feeling that what we have is no longer good enough. While some possessions are necessary to address fundamental human needs in order to move beyond survival (stuff related to shelter, nourishment and love), the initial joy of any possession fades. This is why buying stuff doesn't lead to happiness nor the sense that you ever have enough. After a while, the possession becomes something you take for granted as if you've always had it, and you don't notice it as new or good anymore. Marketers know how our brains work, and I suspect you'll begin to be more aware of language that conditions your brain to adapt. For example, in the real estate industry, a smaller house is considered a "starter home." We don't think twice about this term, but in reality we are buying into the the idea that the house is fine to get started in life, but in a few years, the starter home is no longer sufficient.

OUR BRAINS SUCCUMB TO THE HEADWIND/TAILWIND EFFECT: We are more impacted by negative circumstances and challenges that stand in our way, and we tend to be less aware of the good circumstances when things are going our way. A household budget is a good way to illustrate. In spite of having a high degree of certainty in predicting both household income and expenses. Unexpected car repairs, medical bills, a leaky roof or other urgent matters trigger stress, anxiety and survival mode mentality and can immediately overshadow the contingency planning you've done to accommodate any unexpected expenses. In general, we tend to overestimate the cost of negative challenges in our way and underestimate the benefit of positive circumstances that are helping us. This extends to how we envision future possibilities, too. When we look to the future, we tend to overestimate the potential of negative events unfolding and underestimate the potential of positive events unfolding. This is all compounded by rumination, a tendency that is easy to slip into without even being aware, which further imprisons people in a survival mindset.

OUR BRAINS REALLY DON'T LIKE A LOT OF CHOICE: This may seem counterintuitive, but we know from research that people who have a lot of choice when making purchases are much less satisfied with their purchase as compared to people with fewer choices. Whether you're looking for toothpaste, candles (as did the people in the research study) or air conditioners, we are inundated with options. While on the surface it appears as though choice would improve satisfaction, because we get to buy exactly what we want, when we have a lot of choice our brains somehow can't forget everything back at the store. This seems to generate regret over what we did not buy. This leaves us back in a survival mindset focused on what we don't have.

MONEY CAN BUY HAPPINESS

Whoever said "Money can't buy happiness" is partially correct. What researchers have discovered is that when you spend money on experiences, or on things that represent your identity, you're more likely to be happy. For example, experiences include things like a family vacation, dinner with your partner, giving an employee a family movie night pass, attending a concert with coworkers, or volunteering as a coach or helper. Things that represent your identity might be a vintage acoustic guitar if you like playing music, a rare stamp if you're a philatelist, or a sewing machine that does complex stitches if you're a dress maker.

While spending on stuff will in all likelihood leave you struggling on the treadmill of surviving (because you adapt to the new stuff), spending on experiences or your genuine identity can help you thrive. The key is to be aware of and grateful for every purchase so that it helps reorient you upward toward a thriving mindset.

The ways you save and give money are also connected to your leadership mindset. Like spending money, saving and giving are not reserved for the rich. If they were, then

Thriving Leadership and living a thriving life would be reserved for only the rich, which is not the case. There's still a lot to learn from science about money and happiness, but we do know that grateful people are more generous. From this generosity comes immense joy and happiness. The research I completed in this area uncovered that a deep sense of gratitude was at the core of why generous people from across the income spectrum gave their time, their money and their expertise to help others. I'll leave the advice on the appropriate level of giving, saving and spending as an important task for you and your financial planner. Suffice it to say, how you spend, give and save your money is a reflection of who you are and what you stand for as a leader.

THE TENDENCY TO COMPARE

Our brains love to compare, but I've seldom found that comparing serves me well. There are two general types of comparisons: upward comparisons and downward comparisons.

An upward comparison is when your experiences or possessions compare unfavourably to those of someone else. For example, "The vacations we take are not as nice as the vacations the Jones family takes and the places they visit." Upward comparisons focus on what you don't have (i.e. the Jones' vacations) and leave you feeling and believing that you don't have enough. This is typical of a surviving mindset and living in survival mode. Upward comparisons devalue your circumstances and fail to truly appreciate what you have, be it possessions, relationships or circumstances.

A downward comparison is when you come out of the comparison favourably. This is when your comparison stacks up something of yours against someone else's that is worse than yours (at least in your opinion). For example, after receiving a diagnosis of hypothyroidism (a very common, lifelong condition that requires medication), you might say, "At least I don't have cancer like Pat." It might seem innocent enough, but these comparisons rely on someone else clearly losing out. Other examples of downward comparisons are "I couldn't imagine living the way they do in parts of the developing world where they don't have running water." Or "I couldn't imagine what my life would be like if I could not walk or was confined to a wheelchair."

You may read or hear some advice to use a downward comparison in order to be grateful. Although it would unlikely use the term "downward comparison," the advice generally encourages you to think of people who are less fortunate than you regarding a given situation or circumstance. If that's the only way you can find something to be grateful for, fine, but I discourage you from making downward comparisons in order to find gratitude. Comparing is a roundabout way to see something as a gift, and I recommend using it only as a last resort, as sometimes I have.

The reasons downward comparisons should be used as the last resort to find gratitude are:

THERE IS A LACK OF FOCUS ON WHAT YOU POSSESS.
The primary focus becomes what others don't have. And if the only reason you're grateful is because others don't have something, this conditional gratitude will make it very difficult for your gratitude to be permanent. For example, what happens when those you compare yourself to have more, or for some reason you have less (or get diagnosed with cancer like Pat)? How will you find gratitude?

IT INFERS A JUDGMENT OF OTHERS AND WHAT THEY POSSESS AS NOT WORTHY OF GRATITUDE, AT LEAST NOT FOR YOU.

This easily happens when someone from the developed world experiences what it is like to live in the developing world. I believe everyone is able to be grateful in virtually any circumstance. Downward comparisons go against the core belief: "I am worthy and have much to be grateful for." This belief applies to everyone. That said, I won't tell someone they should be grateful for a situation. That would be judgmental; they need to find the gratitude themselves. Similarly, I wouldn't tell them what is off-limits for gratitude. Again, it's their job to figure it out for themselves.

WE RUN THE RISK OF OBJECTIFYING PEOPLE AND TREATING THEM WITHOUT DIGNITY.

For example, if you're grateful for what you have because of your circumstances over theirs, is it still possible they can be grateful for their circumstance? I believe yes. But using a house as an example, how would you feel telling someone you are grateful for your home because it is so much nicer than theirs?

The best way to continually move toward thriving so you're not slipping into surviving is to practice gratitude. The simple practice of making a gratitude list is a huge step up in the direction toward a thriving mindset.

For seven chapters I've been hammering away at the idea of making a gratitude list. This is the fundamental habit for Thriving Leadership and living a thriving life. You will find you have good days and bad days. You will have days where your gratitude list will flow freely and you'll have days where you'll struggle to list one thing. The key is perseverance. Just keep going.

PERSEVERING IN MY BUSINESS

In 2011, I received a call from a potential client, Matt, about speaking at an upcoming conference in about two months. It was local, so I set up a meeting where we discussed what he wanted to achieve, and I discovered that someone had recommended me to him. We had a great meeting and I felt it was a slam dunk because of the referral. Two weeks passed and I hadn't heard a thing. "Oh no, how did it go sideways?" I called and emailed numerous times and eventually I heard back, "We're going with someone else this year. Thanks for taking time to meet with us." I was disappointed, but decided I'd stay in touch with him.

Almost five years later, in 2016, I got a phone call on a Friday night. "Hi Steve, it's Matt. What are you doing tomorrow?"

"What do you mean?" I said.

Matt said, "We've got our conference this weekend, and our opening keynote speaker is stuck and can't make it. Are you available?"

"Of course I am. I need you to swing by the house so we can knock this out of the park."

After our meeting, as Matt was leaving the house, I said, "This is the quickest piece of business I've ever got."

He said, "I don't think so. Over the past five years you've stayed in touch with me. You've sent me relevant articles. You've called and emailed. Most of the time I didn't even call you back. So when the conference lost the speaker who was booked by head office, only one person came to mind: you!" He asked me to share the story of perseverance with the team as an example of not giving up.

I reviewed my customer tracking system and found we had three meetings and I had sent him one book, one card, two proposals, 10 articles and 14 emails, and I left 13 voicemails.

I don't know if he returned a voicemail or not, but I decided to persist in adding value through my outreach. I'd smile when leaving a message and I never tried to use guilt or shame to get him to call back. Doing this follow-up was neither easy nor hard once I made the commitment I was going to stay in touch with him. It's the same when you commit to making a gratitude list every day. Once you're committed, the fact is that some days are easy and some are hard is irrelevant. I've been making a gratitude list for about 12 years and I haven't missed a day since 2011. Some days are easy and some days I struggle. I struggle because of the challenges of life and from the mundanity of my gratitudes at times.

I know that this daily gratitude practice has been a game changer for me in my personal life and in my business. While I've always been a positive person, I spend much less time with a surviving mindset and much more time with a thriving mindset, which is where I want to be.

I encourage you to make the commitment to make your gratitude list every single day. We're going to talk about the gratitude list more in Chapter 9 but for now, get started if you haven't already, and if you've already started the habit, keep it up.

SEVENTH LAW OF GRATEFUL LEADERSHIP

A THRIVING MINDSET IS LIKE A GARDEN: IT MUST BE CARED FOR

IMPLICATIONS FOR YOU:
If you don't consciously and intentionally develop your gratitude muscles, they will atrophy and you will fall downward to the surviving mindset.

Where your life goes, your leadership example follows. The same holds for those you lead, so you need to continuously monitor and support them.

You must continuously reorient yourself toward a thriving mindset, and it is by gratefully acknowledging the good in your life that you overcome the unrelenting force. When you realize that indeed, "I have enough! And it is a gift!" you have uncovered the secret to a thriving mindset.

ASK YOURSELF THE FOLLOWING QUESTIONS:

When does negativity most often dominate my mindset?

How often do I ruminate over all the good going on in my life and all the people who are helping me?

How can I better spend, save and give money in ways that reflect the person I am becoming?

What do I think about the idea of not doing downward comparisons to find gratitude?

How can I ensure that I am persistently working on my gratitude muscles?

KNOWING WHAT I KNOW, WHAT DO I TAKE AWAY FROM THIS CHAPTER?

CHAPTER 8

DEALING WITH CHALLENGES

IT WAS APRIL 4TH, 2013. We got a phone call from my sister at five a.m. that Mom had been rushed to the hospital and that we better get down to the emergency room quickly. She died within the hour, and fortunately, most of the family was with her. My brother Greg and his family arrived just after Mom died. Mom's brother Tony and our daughter Stef, who both lived in Toronto, arrived in Halifax the next day. It was a sad time for me. Mom was a very special person in my life. I am grateful she died peacefully, which is a blessing because I had been anticipating a very uncomfortable death for Mom.

As previously mentioned, Mom was a smoker and she loved her cigarettes. Mom was in her late fifties when she kicked the habit.

For the last five years of her life she was plagued by COPD, which is effectively hardening of the lungs. COPD is irreversible damage caused by long-term smoking, and while they can try to slow its progress and deal with the symptoms of the disease, COPD continually makes breathing ever more difficult.

About 18 months prior to her death, she had a critical

incident that left her gasping for breath. Dad called an ambulance which whisked her to the emergency room and the family was called in. I had never seen someone I love in such pain. Mom could barely breathe. For 45 minutes I watched helplessly as Mom fought for every breath. It was as if she was breathing through a crumpled straw that was being tightly squeezed. Doctors and nurses were running about and methodically escalating their response to Mom's situation. The look in Mom's eyes scared me; the thought of it still gives me a sick feeling in my stomach. Eventually, they brought in a ventilator. Before applying it, they explained that it was a temporary measure, the last they could apply to help her, and that, if she didn't respond, there would be nothing more they could do. They hoped that the ventilator would stabilize her breathing so that they could administer other treatments. They emphasized that, in her condition, there was no guarantee. They would give her a day or two on the ventaltor, and hope after that she could breathe on her own. While I was grateful that the doctors and nurses were able to stabilize Mom, I was struggling to find gratitude. But I looked, and was able to find good in the situation—most notably, being part of a loving, supportive family.

Mom had a "no resuscitate" order as part of her instructions and wanted no artificial means to keep her alive on a permanent basis. This meant that when they removed the ventilator, if she couldn't breathe on her own, we would be looking at her final days. It was so scary the day they removed the ventilator, and fortunately, for Mom and for us, she was able to breathe on her own. For the next couple days one of us was with her around the clock. Her life changed from that day onward because of the increased concoction of medications she had to take.

That day, watching her gasp for air, was extremely painful for me. It is indelibly stamped on my mind and in hindsight it prepared me for her death in ways that I did not anticipate. After this incident, I feared Mom would die a horrific, painful death gasping for air. That did not happen, and for that I am grateful.

As we walked out of the emergency room on April 4th I no longer had a mom. At least not one I could turn to and hug or ask for help. Dad and her five kids divvied up the arrangements that quickly had to be dealt with. I had to deal with the funeral home and contact a few family members. By ten a.m. I had everything done. There was nothing else to do that day but feel the sorrow. As all of this was unfolding, in the back of my mind was a major client commitment for which I had to make a decision. I was scheduled to speak for a client to close out their conference in Halifax that afternoon. The client knew my mom really well, as he grew up with her. As I was thinking about what to do, I received an email from him offering his condolences and understanding if I couldn't speak to his team.

On top of the heartache that overwhelmed me, I was in a conundrum. While some may think, "Your mom died, this is a no-brainer; stay home with your family," the answer wasn't that simple for me. I had worked with this client for a long time and helped them put together their conference program. There was nothing else for me to do that day in preparation for Mom's funeral and everyone else was busy taking care of their responsibilities. Should I speak? Or should I gracefully ask to be excused? What would Mom want me to do? If I said yes, would it be disrespectful to Mom? And if I said yes, would I be able to hold myself together because I would be sharing my personal story? I felt I couldn't answer this without some help. I spoke with Dad and Lyn. My father and my wife were very supportive and gave me a much needed perspective that I wasn't going to find on my own.

They made me realize that the next 24 hours would pass whether I spoke at the event or not. Yes, I could simply do nothing, as life isn't always about being productive and doing things. However, the work I do with gratitude is the gift I provide in the world, one which Mom nurtured, grew and encouraged in me.

It is a wonderful gift to have non-judgmental support, and ultimately they felt it was a decision best made by me.

I also shared with them what was haunting me in the back of my mind. It was the stark reality that if I didn't work, I wouldn't get paid. While it seems crass to talk about working because of the money on the day my mom died, I had to talk about it, because I didn't want to regret whatever would be decided. The bottom line was that if I didn't speak at the event, then I wouldn't be getting paid, in spite of the fact that I put in all the work except the hour that I was scheduled to speak. And there was no guarantee that we would reschedule for next year or that my topic would fit with the theme of any future conference. All of this was unfolding at a time when my business was in a downturn. I definitely didn't want to do this for the wrong reasons, and if I did it just for the money, I knew I would regret it for the rest of my life.

In the end, I decided to speak at the event. There wasn't much time to make the decision, and fortunately I still think it was the right choice. Only the company owners knew about Mom's death and I asked that they not share it with anyone. I was not looking for sympathy nor any special attention. After all, my purpose in being there was for them so that they could understand the transformative power of living a grateful life and being a grateful leader.

The death of a loved one or trauma can cause a numbness in the midst of the pain and ache. While the numbness was there, I could feel my mom's presence beside me during my presentation (and still now at this moment as I write). My session went over very well. A group of serious, hard-working men (and it was all men) laughed and joked and took time to savour the good things in life. Our session worked. I stuck around for dinner with them but left before dessert. As you might expect, I just wasn't feeling in a celebratory mood.

We had a beautiful funeral celebration for Mom and saw hundreds of family and friends over the next few days. Looking back, I can see that I was numb through it; I'm certain that helped me cope. With the funeral behind me, I just wanted to relax on the weekend. I was cooking in the kitchen, which I love doing, and turned on music. Lyn walked into the kitchen as a 70's song came on. I can't remember the name, other than it was one of the defining songs of my adolescence. With each beat of the music, I could feel something welling up inside my body. I looked at Lyn and was overcome with emotion. I collapsed in her arms and bawled uncontrollably. It was cathartic. At that moment, I knew Mom was with me and would always be with me. The form in which she was with me was much different than how I had ever experienced her presence before, but she was there. I get to see her regularly as her burial plot is in our neighbourhood and her voice is still on Dad's outgoing voicemail message.

More recently, I've been working with a client who is making gratitude a central element of their culture. Colleen is a member of a leadership team and has risen from within her organization to become the gratitude ambassador across the entire organization. We are in touch on a regular basis and from my perspective Colleen has been a real gift to her colleagues and the clients they serve.

After about a year of gratitude work with the leadership team, the decision was made to involve the rest of the staff and introduce them to the power of gratitude. We did this through multiple half-day introductory sessions. I didn't know who would attend each session and, to my delight, Colleen was at the first session.

As we mingled over coffee before getting started, she shared, "I'm having a really hard time with my gratitudes."

Without batting an eye I said, "That's perfect. Do you think you're special and you're the only one who will have it easy?" While what I said is a universal truth, I wouldn't be this abrupt with just anyone, but Colleen and I had a relationship.

She laughed and said, "I guess you're right. That makes total sense."

After the session I approached Colleen and asked, "So what's going on that's making it difficult?"

She shared that some people very close to her were in the midst of very serious health challenges, that it was getting the best of her and she couldn't stop thinking about it. When the people we love are suffering or dealing with health issues, it should occupy our minds; however, it needn't keep us feeling trapped in survival mode. Colleen was crying now.

I asked, "Is there any good in what's going on? That's what gratitude is about. It's not about ignoring or dismissing the challenges your loved ones face. It's about finding the genuine good in the situation."

She looked up and said, "Well, we have great health care and they are getting the best care possible. And as for me, imagine the state I would be in if I wasn't doing my gratitudes?"

I encouraged her to persist with the daily practice. On the difficult days, I told her to look for simple things: hot tea, the warm sun, a friendly dog on the way to work. And don't be too hard on yourself. If you miss a day, don't worry about it. Give yourself a break.

We will all have times when finding gratitude will be difficult. We must trust and believe that "the good" is out there, whether we see it or not. We must persist in looking for it.

And then there are the daily challenges that don't compare to the loss of a loved one. Some are trivial and some are significant. I had the privilege in chairing a university board, which was a very challenging and eye-opening experience. Universities are complex; the fact that the university I had volunteered to help happened to be the smallest one in the province didn't seem to make it any less complex. Early in my role as Chair we were navigating some challenging times and working with management to ensure the fiscal sustainability of the school. We established a small task group of the Board with some external advisors to explore several very sensitive options. The Board was divided on the need to establish the task group and was usually divided on any of the work the group completed. While creative conflict is very helpful, because it prevents groupthink, this was not the case with us. I could see how it was dividing our board. It was almost is if we had those in favour and those against, and factions were forming along those lines.

The task group had come to a point in their work where they had to bring a recommendation to the board. The external advisors, who as experts in their fields were all volunteering their time to the effort, were also aware of the division within the board. This made me uncomfortable because I didn't want them to think we didn't appreciate their work and contribution. Every Board member felt that way, regardless of their position on the sensitive issues. It was decided to invite the entire task group to a portion of the board meeting to support the group's presentation, because we wanted experts in the room to answer any questions.

I remember the day of the board meeting well, because we called a Special Meeting of the Board, which may have been the first in the university's history. I was very anxious.

How would the task group be treated? How would Board members act? What would the Board ultimately decide? These were all troubling me. I wasn't the only one concerned. Other members of the Board shared their anxieties with me, too.

To make matters worse, I was late for the meeting. Chair, and 10 minutes late. As I was driving to the meeting, I called ahead to let them know I'd be late and ask that they wait for me. I also decided we would do something I had never done with this board before but I had done countless times with my clients. I decided that at the opening of the meeting when we go around the table to introduce ourselves, that we would each share one thing we are grateful for.

I arrived and the room was abuzz. People were standing up and everyone was talking in small groups aligned with their interest. Including the task group and senior leadership team, there were more than two dozen people in the room. I could feel the skepticism when I announced my idea. I could see them doing the mental math: 30 people times 30-60 seconds for each gratitude; this is going to take 20-30 minutes. Practically speaking, most people want to get straight to the work. They have the attitude, "Let's get at it!" This belief is especially prevalent when the issue or work at hand is going to take a lot of time.

I started and shared. I don't remember what gratitude I shared, but I was inspired and uplifted by the gratitudes others shared. As we rounded the table, the gratitudes included the respect people had for their Board colleagues, love for their families, the freedoms we enjoy, the students we get to serve, the support received from mentors throughout a career, the volunteers on the task group and several around personal health.

I thought the exercise went well because the conversation around the task group's work was exceptional. Board members pressed for clarity but were respectful, and ultimately the Board approved the recommendation made by the task group. And while the recommendation was not unanimously approved, we left the meeting room with one plan and one voice.

I felt good about the outcome but was not certain if the gratitude exercise had any impact, because no one said anything about it. The next day, I received a phone call from Bill. He was one of the external experts on the task group. Bill was a no-nonsense type of guy and because of his demeanor someone might incorrectly describe him as irritable or grouchy. He said, "I was at the meeting 20 minutes early and because you were late, I don't know if you had realized it or not, but the tension in the room was so high you could cut it with a knife." He went on. "Steve, in my 45 years in this business I had never seen anyone do something like that gratitude thing you did with us last night. At first I was thinking 'Why are you doing this?' but today I know why. It totally changed the atmosphere in the room. It totally changed the room. In all my years, I have never before seen a transformation like what happened last night. I just thought you'd want to know."

I appreciated Bill's call and, in particular, his reminder that my actions made a difference. Up until that point, I had only met Bill at a couple of briefings, and we hadn't spoken about anything other than the project at hand. It would have been much easier for him to do nothing; he had to go out of his way to find my phone number. While I can't be certain, I think Bill's call was motivated out of the gratitude that he experienced. Gratitude has the power to do that.

As we covered in Chapter 7, the brain's hyper-sensitivity to negative circumstances makes it extremely hard to see and find the good in difficult or adverse situations. Challenges and negativity trigger your reptilian brain which induces fear and stress. This diminishes your brain's executive function and moves you downward to survival mindset decision making: fight, flight or freeze. But gratitude truly is the equalizer. It is the antidote. It is the catalyst for positive action. It negates the stress response and is the source of a thriving mindset and ultimately a thriving life.

Gratitude shifts you from fear to love, from scarcity to abundance. Gratitude unlocks you from freezing by inspiring you into action. Gratitude moves you forward toward what you want so you don't run from what you have. Gratitude is the path to freedom.

THE TAKEAWAY

In the midst of challenges it is difficult to be grateful, however it is during these difficult times that gratitude has the potential to help us more than we can ever imagine. I remember once reading, "It's easy to be happy when everything is going your way." It's true, and it's equally easy to be grateful when everything is popping up roses. True character is visible in both good times and in bad times through unwavering beliefs, not whimsical feelings.

There are a few things you can do if you want to thrive when you're facing challenges. The secret is in finding the good. It doesn't mean you ignore the crap, you just need to get your eyes off of the crap long enough so that you can see some of the good that is there. Here are three tips to help you deal with the crap in your life:

The best measure is to build a strong gratitude practice which will insulate you from the challenge. This took years for me to do, and I'm still not perfect, because I still can succumb to the drain of a challenge. The best time to build your gratitude practice is 20 years ago. The second best time is today.

The next best thing I recommend is to read or listen to someone else's gratitudes. It is a non-judgmental way to regain perspective and reorient yourself toward a thriving mindset. Whoever is writing or listing their gratitudes has no agenda nor are they trying to convince you of anything. There is amazing power in not deeply knowing who is sharing the gratitudes. It can sometimes feel like you're being told to be grateful when you talk to someone you know or love (who knows your situation) and they talk about what they're grateful for. For me, I've read a gratitude blog for the past seven or eight years, and I find it a great way to regain perspective. When I read Lisa's blog talking about her days as an alcoholic, her recovery from breast cancer, her long training runs with her husband or her time with her grandchildren, there are days I think she is writing it specifically for me. But I know there's no way that's possible. I feel the same non-judgmental inspiration when I read the thousands of gratitudes posted on The Daily Gratitudes page which is hosted on our Gratitude at Work website at www.gratitudeatwork.ca/daily. On this page you can subscribe to a weekday email that has six gratitudes—three from me and three from our weekly guest contributor. Take a moment to subscribe now. It can be life-changing.

Thirdly, I encourage you to look back on your life and identify a major challenge you overcame. It could be an educational achievement, a health scare, or the tragic loss of a loved one. It truly doesn't matter what it is as long as, in your mind, you consider overcoming it as a major accomplishment. For this challenge, identify what you're grateful for about it today. You'll likely identify things you were not grateful for at the time. Then ask yourself, "How do I make sense of my current challenge in light of the major challenge(s) I've overcome in my life?" Use this to find the good in the challenge you face today. You can also turn to other people you trust and ask them about challenges they've overcome and then ask them what they're now grateful for as they look back.

The harsh reality is that no one is free from the challenges of life. As gut wrenching as they may be, we should not allow ourselves to use them as an excuse to justify a surviving mindset. The Eighth Law of Grateful Leadership should be no surprise, and while it is pretty simple, it is absolutely critical that you find ways to discover the good in your challenges.

EIGHTH LAW OF GRATEFUL LEADERSHIP

CRAP STILL HAPPENS

IMPLICATIONS FOR YOU:
When crap happens in your life, you need gratitude the most. Be on the constant lookout for good, especially for the good in the challenges you face.

Try to find the good in every situation as quickly as possible. The quicker, the better. The more you practice gratitude, the more conditioned your thriving mindset will be, and the easier it gets to find the good quickly.

Consume, by reading or listening to, other people's gratitudes.

ASK YOURSELF THE FOLLOWING QUESTIONS:

What are the biggest challenges I've overcome in my life?

When I reflect on the biggest challenges I've overcome, what am I grateful for?

In what challenges am I having difficulty finding the good?

Who do I know who has dealt with a lot of crap in their life, and yet seems to maintain a thriving mindset? What can I learn from them?

KNOWING WHAT I KNOW, WHAT DO I TAKE AWAY FROM THIS CHAPTER?

CHAPTER 9

IT'S NOT A QUICK FIX

WHILE IT SOUNDS LIKE a cliché, it is true. Living a thriving life is a journey, not a destination. Spending more time thriving and less time surviving requires daily effort. Thriving is not onerous work but it does take conscious attention each and every day. You will still face challenges and at times find yourself in situations you'd only describe as chaos. And it's unlikely you will suddenly wake up one morning to find yourself thriving. It's gradual, so be patient

A couple of years ago, Lyn and I booked a week on Cape Cod and in The Berkshires, where we were going to catch a James Taylor concert on July 4th. Dating back to the 80's we've always treasured our vacations in New England, and it is close enough to Nova Scotia that we always drove. This trip was no different. We were heading out on the Saturday of the Canada Day long weekend (Canadian holiday on Monday), so Friday night I cleaned the car inside and out. I love travelling in a clean car. We were up early ready for a 6:30 a.m. departure. The car was loaded and ready to go except that when I turned the key, nothing. The battery was dead. I couldn't figure it out, as there were some external signal lights dimly lit. I called CAA and they had a tow truck there in 15 minutes. The mechanic eventually discovered the switch on the steering column was on. Turns out I inadvertently switched it on while cleaning the car the night before and it was a bright evening so I didn't notice the exterior car lights. The battery wouldn't hold a charge, so after we got a boost, we headed straight to our service station for a new battery. They graciously fit us into a very busy schedule, which you'd expect on the first long weekend of the summer, and by 11:30 a.m. we were on our way.

As we were driving by the city of Moncton, NB, about two and a half hours into our planned eight hour drive that day, one of the rear side windows of the car shattered. It sounded like a mini-explosion and glass was everywhere in the back seat and throughout the wagon's rear storage space. I couldn't believe it—there was no explanation. Fortunately, we were close to a city, so we pulled into Moncton and stopped at the first store to ask for directions to the nearest glass repair shop. Lyn hopped out of the car and headed into the store. It wasn't five seconds and Lyn was back in the car. Blood was all over her foot, and she said, "Get me to the hospital." She had tripped on a piece of rusted steel rebar protruding from the parking lot that would have once secured a concrete curb in place. First the battery, now this. I couldn't believe it! Lyn said, "Drop me at the emergency and you go get the window fixed." Fortunately the hospital was less than three minutes away. I dropped her at the emergency department and headed over to the glass repair shop. They were very busy. Remember, it's a Saturday afternoon of the first long weekend of summer. They checked their parts system and could locate only one replacement window in the entire country—in Saskatchewan. "It'll take at least three days to get here."

"You've got to be kidding," I thought.

He said, "What if we clean out your car, secure plastic over the window, and we'll call you when the glass arrives?"

I said, "OK, but we're not from Moncton. We're on our way to Cape Cod and we'll be on our way through again in about a week. Could you replace it then?"

"Yup."

We had a plan. They had me out in about 20 minutes and I headed over to the emergency. It was packed. Lyn was in a wheelchair and as soon as I sat down, they called her name. They gave her a bunch of shots in case of infection and they sewed her toe back together with a few stitches. In 40 minutes we walked out with a prescription for pain and instructions that she had to keep the foot dry—no swimming nor walks on the beach. We arrived at our final destination in Bangor that night, a few hours later than planned and exhausted. We were both so tired, the wine we thought we needed still half-filled our glasses when we woke the next morning.

The next morning was glorious. Lyn's foot was sore, but she could walk slowly. We stopped at a mall, where she picked up some footwear that was comfortable. After arriving in Hyannisport we booked our ferry tickets for a day trip to Nantucket the next day. Although we didn't break any land records walking around town, we enjoyed a glorious day and learned lots about the island and its central role in the whaling industry. On the ferry ride back home after dinner, we were on the outside deck enjoying the views. About 20 minutes in, the wind picked up, the fog rolled in and I was getting chilly and we were getting wet. I said to Lyn, "I'm heading inside." When I got to the door, I heard Lyn scream. When I turned around she was lying on the floor of the ferry. I ran over. She was in intense pain and could hardly speak. She had slipped and fallen on the steel armrest of a chair. The ferry's crew was very helpful and did what they could to comfort her. Lyn was in shock and in a lot of pain. When the ferry docked, an ambulance was waiting for her. Everyone disembarked and we were whisked to the Hyannisport Emergency Department, our second trip to the ER in less than a week. We were there for a few hours. An x-ray confirmed that Lyn broke four ribs. The doctor said the only treatment for broken ribs was pain medication. We got a cab back to our hotel at three a.m. and picked up another pain medication. This one was much more potent: Oxycontin. Lyn barely got out of bed the next day, but by evening she was able to sit up and was actually hungry. We had two more days on Cape Cod before heading to The Berkshires for James Taylor, and we wondered whether we should go or just head home. Should Lyn just hop on a plane and fly home? On day two, she was up and around and I couldn't believe it; she was game for the concert. Day three was a four or five hour drive to Western Massachusetts, during which she slept. When we arrived, Lyn's spirits were perked by the large outlet mall that welcomed us at our highway exit.

Although she was uncomfortable for the rest of the trip and in particular sitting in a small chair at the concert, Lyn was the model of positivity and hope. She even got in four hours of shopping at the outlet mall. On the way home through Moncton, the car glass was replaced and we arrived home without incident later that afternoon.

When I shared our adventure, one of my best friends, Derek, said, "There's a moral to your story."

I said, "Really?"

He said, "Yeah, don't wash your car before you go on vacation."

Seriously, overall it was a great trip: time in the car with Lyn, the concert, beautiful scenery, much needed medical care (and all insured), and the list goes on.

Our journey to New England is like the journey of

life. When Lyn tripped on that rusty piece of rebar, I didn't immediately think, "I'm grateful that she nearly ripped her toe off." And I still don't. What I tried to do as quickly as possible was find the good. Lyn and I talked about it. How fortunate that the hospital was close by, that it was very fast, and that the nurses and doctors who cared for her were kind and knew exactly what to do. This one was fairly easy to find the good.

When Lyn fell on the ferry, it was more difficult to find the good. But we did find good. The support from the ferry company, the paramedics who carried her off the boat, the nearby emergency room at 11 p.m., the professional care and quick diagnosis, the pain medication, and the fact that we had travel insurance to cover the costs.

When we woke up each morning on that trip, we had to continually remind ourselves that there was good around us. When we saw people doing the things we had planned to do on that vacation, things like swimming in a pool, riding bikes along a trail or walking along the beach, we had to remind ourselves that there was good around us.

While I've always known that living a grateful life is a journey and not a destination, this New England vacation re-inforced for me that gratitude is not a destination. When it comes to our personal development, we never arrive and we are never done, at least if we are striving for excellence. There's always something to work on, and for building a grateful frame of mind, the reason is simple. Because in life, crap hap-pens, and it's most likely to happen when you least expect it. A vacation gone sideways, the unexpected death of a loved one, or a disruption that makes your business obsolete, or an-other negative event can easily overcome your efforts. They alter your dominant mindset, reverting you back to survival mindset and the struggle that accompanies being stuck there.

Building a grateful frame of mind isn't a quick fix, either.

You need to put in the work to develop a thriving mindset and continuously reorient yourself toward thriving. You will notice improvements in your mindset almost immediately, but depending on your circumstances, it may take months or years before you truly spend most of your time thriving.

Through my professional practice, my primary research and the body of literature on gratitude, I have distilled the many different gratitude practices into four simple habits. I call them the happiness habits, because that's what they'll do: give you genuine happiness. These habits are simple and will take only about four to eight minutes per day.

These habits make an ungrateful person or ingrateful person a grateful person, and they make a grateful person a more grateful person. And, as mentioned, they are deceptively simple. You may already be doing them today, consciously or unconsciously, but your goal in the future is to do them consciously and automatically.

HABIT 1: MAKE A LIST OF WHAT YOU'RE GRATEFUL FOR

This is the most studied gratitude habit in the literature. Making a list of gratitudes contributes to overall well-being and your physical and mental health. Simply make a list of three things you're grateful for and record it daily.

HERE ARE 20 TIPS TO HELP YOU MAKE A GRATITUDE LIST:

1. **Use a journal every day:** Use a journal to make your gratitude list. It could be a physical journal or some type of electronic journal. The physical act of writing does more for you than simply thinking about what you're grateful for.

2. **Pick a time that works for you:** When making your gratitude list, find a time of day that works in your schedule. It might be first thing in the morning, or before you go to bed or maybe at lunch. While I generally make my gratitude list at the end of the day, it doesn't matter when you make your list; you just need a time where you can step back for a few minutes.

3. **Pick a place to write and put your journal there:** This is important to set yourself up for success. For example, if you're making your list at night just before you go to sleep, then you might want to put your journal on your bedside table. One person I know keeps her journal in her car because she writes her list while waiting for her kids after school at the bus stop. Again, it doesn't matter where you write your list. Make it convenient and you're more likely to keep going. If you use an electronic journal, set up a notification to remind you.

4. **Think of someone who stands out in your day:** Oftentimes the biggest challenge many people have with the daily practice of writing a gratitude list is simply getting started. One way to get started on your list is to ask yourself, "Who stood out in my day yesterday?" Use the answer to begin your list of what you're grateful for.

5. **Single out the best part of your day:** Think back over your day and find the part you wouldn't want to do without, or you couldn't do without. This is another great way to get started on your gratitude list. Then, use the best part of your day to kick-start your list.

6. **Include different areas of your life:** I often include one thing I'm grateful for from my personal life, one

from my work life and one from the community in which I live. You could draw from other areas such as spiritual, health, financial, professional, and even more specific relational areas: friends, family and romantic.

7. **It's OK if you miss a day:** Don't beat yourself up if you miss a day. Writing a gratitude list is supposed to bring out the best in you, so if you miss a day, don't get all worked up about it. Recommit and get back at it tomorrow.

8. **List gratitudes in terms of benefits and sacrifices:** Frame more of your gratitudes in terms of what others have done (i.e. farmers who persevered) as compared to how you benefit (i.e. food on the table). Based on my analysis, on average we are four times more likely to express our gratitudes in terms of benefits to us as opposed to the sacrifices of others. There's nothing wrong with this, but by including more sacrifices in your gratitudes, you will deepen your connection to others and focus more on others, which is a critical social skill.

9. **Draw on a recent accomplishment:** Look back over the last few weeks and think of an accomplishment. It could be one of yours or that of someone close to you, perhaps your team or maybe someone in your family. Then list the people involved in helping bring about the accomplishment.

10. **Use vivid, meaningful language:** Writing your gratitude list shouldn't be a rote exercise. Whenever possible, use words that truly convey the feeling of your gratitude. For example, instead of, "I'm grateful for an ample supply of food," write, "I'm grateful for garden fresh vegetables and the smell of our kitchen and the privilege of knowing I won't go to bed

hungry." While both gratitudes are perfectly fine, the latter triggers more of your genuine emotions and helps you better experience gratitude.

11. **Wind back the clock and come forward:** You've come through so much. Think back to your childhood, then follow your life through your adolescent years and up to now. Recall the activities and the people in all the different phases of your life and reflect on how they shaped the person you've become.

12. **Look for mentors:** Maybe it's your parents, a teacher, a coach, a boss, whomever. Think of the people who've played key a role in your life and in your development.

13. **The last sixty minutes is all that counts:** Make your gratitude list by looking at the last sixty minutes only. Nothing further back than one hour. While it may sound difficult, it will quickly remind you of many blessings that are easy to miss.

14. **Don't force it:** If you find yourself sitting and trying to write your gratitudes but nothing is coming out, don't force it. If you find writing your list is becoming a chore, then take a day off and come back fresh. Research has proven that gratitude decreases when we try to force it.

15. **Look back through your journal:** One of the best ways to remind yourself of what you're grateful for is to go back and read through what you wrote last week or the week before. It's OK to list something again—you might use the same language, or you may try some more vivid, meaningful words.

16. **Learn from a recent challenge:** The challenges you've faced and the ones you've overcome define your character. Identify a challenge you've recently moved through; it may be personal or professional.

Reflect on what you discovered from the experience. Start your gratitude list there.

17. **Go deeper:** This technique is helpful when you already have one item written on your gratitude list. Consider what you've listed and go deeper with it. For this one item, think about why you're grateful for it, all the people to whom you're grateful, what they did, and perhaps most importantly, why they did it—try to understand their motivations. Add more gratitudes based on what comes up.

18. **Ask someone:** Ask a person you trust, "If you were me, what would you be grateful for?" You might be surprised by the answer.

19. **Pay attention to annoyances:** Hard to believe, but it's true. Take your annoyances and transform them into something you're grateful for. For example, "Damn, I burnt the toast" turns into: "I'm grateful for 1) modern conveniences like my toaster, 2) the sense of smell and taste, which provide pleasure but also keep me safe, and 3) the farmers and producers of the food that makes its way to my table." While gratitude doesn't fix the toast, it reframes the situation for you.

20. **Resist the temptation to think it's stupid:** Writing a gratitude list is so simple, but at some point you may catch yourself thinking that it probably isn't worth the time and effort. It's easy to think that you've got it figured out or you've tapped all the benefits. Resist the temptation to give up making your gratitude list.

HABIT 2: READ OR LISTEN TO WHAT OTHERS ARE GRATEFUL FOR

As mentioned previously, as a leader you need inspiration and fuel. Even you, if you're not careful, can end up being fueled by the crap that surrounds you. Whether it's the unrelenting force, the news, business challenges, or simply the everyday struggles of life, outside influences can quickly get you stuck down in a surviving mindset. Thriving Leaders need a constant supply of perspectives and views that are positive and non-judgmental. When you read or listen to what others are grateful for, you get just that, and it will help keep you oriented toward a thriving mindset. The daily gratitude blog I mentioned that I subscribe to is called Habitual Gratitude, and I highly recommend it no matter your circumstances. In addition, I also read the gratitudes from 10 to 20 people every day. You don't need to do that much, but it can help you spend more time thriving and less time surviving. The easiest way for you to make this habitual is The Daily Gratitudes. Go to www.gratitudeatwork.ca/daily and you'll find thousands of gratitude posts to read. On that page, if you have not already, you can also sign up for The Daily Gratitudes, which will give you six gratitudes to read each weekday morning. I can guarantee the practice of reading other people's gratitudes will help you with your gratitude list, especially on the days when life can feel overwhelming.

HABIT 3: SHARE YOUR GRATITUDES WITH OTHERS

Let the world know what you're grateful for. Sharing gratitudes is a humble acknowledgement of the gifts and blessings you've received. Sharing gratitudes is not about bragging. When you share what you're grateful for, especially what you're genuinely grateful for, the people around you and the people you lead will gradually come to see the real you. They will know what is truly important to you as a Thriving Leader. Your shared gratitudes serve as fuel for others. Do not underestimate the impact you will have through the simple sharing of your gratitudes. This habit strengthens the social bonds you share with others and builds trust. As in any relationship, the more vulnerable and genuine you are, the greater the trust you'll build.

In organizations, I recommend that every meeting begins with the sharing of one gratitude per person. What I like about this exercise is that 1) it gets the meeting started on the right tone, 2) it's extremely simple, and 3) it covers each of the first three habits. Even during the writing of this book on the weekly calls with my writing coach, Alaina, we began our calls with the two of us sharing one thing we were grateful for.

A great way to make Habit 3 habitual is to partner up with someone and share your gratitudes with each other. Clients of mine call it "pick a gratitude buddy." Find someone close to you and make the commitment to share with each other, one to three gratitudes each day. You can email, text, post to social media, phone: it doesn't matter how, just make it something that will work for the two of you. Be accountable to your buddy and hold them accountable.

This habit will truly test your mettle as a Thriving Leader. It's easy to share what you're grateful for when times are good or the situations are rosy. But when times are tough and circumstances are dire, this is when Thriving Leadership is needed most. It's at times like these that we need the reframing power of gratitude. It's easy to fall into the traps of complaining or blaming, however, as a leader you have the ability and responsibility to set an inspiring tone. You do that by seeing the good and helping others see it. Gratitude is the simplest and most effective way I know of doing this. It doesn't mean you ignore the challenges or crap. Certainly, acknowledge the challenging circumstances, but make sure you remind yourself and those you lead that there is good around you and lots to be grateful for. You have a choice with your mindset: be a thermostat or thermometer. Thermometers respond to the temperature in the room and settle out to the existing temperature, while thermostats set the temperature in the room. Thriving Leaders are thermostats that set the temperature in the room. They are the ones who set the example for an inspiring positive culture. Gratitude is at the heart of the thriving mindset which makes it so important for being a positive inspiring example.

For example, yesterday I was golfing with my best friends and it was a beautiful fall day in Nova Scotia. Although it was only about 12 degrees Celsius (~54F), there was not a drop of wind. Conditions were perfect for golf. I struggled on the front half playing one of the worst sets of nine holes I played all season. I could not figure out the speed on the greens, and worse, my game had turned into a series of mis-hit after mis-hit. After eight holes, I had already lost four or five balls in a variety of hazards. While it was frustrating, I was conscious of this frustration. I said to myself, "I'm grateful to be out here playing. I'm out here to have fun, so have fun, and let others around you know you're having fun." I couldn't believe the result. On the frustrating first eight holes, I was 11 over par; on the final ten holes I went four over par. It was the best 10 holes I played all year. While I played a bit over my head and had some lucky breaks on the back nine, I played well because I was relaxed and was enjoying the game, the company of friends and the beauty of nature. I did my best to be a thermostat and while it was tough, I resisted falling into being a thermometer that displayed the level of frustration brought on by my poor play.

HABIT 4: SAY THANK YOU

When I say, "Say thank you," I mean it very broadly. It could be actually saying thank you; it could be a smile; it could be spending time with someone; it could be making or buying a special gift for someone.

You can say thank you back to the person you're grateful to, or you may pay it forward to a complete stranger. Often times much of what I'm grateful for (my freedom, the food on my table, medical care, etc.) I don't know who I should be grateful to or they may have long died. So paying it forward often happens in my life just as I've been on the receiving end of countless people who paid it forward to me.

Saying thank you is the natural external expression of gratitude. When you express gratitude, it's critical to understand the five languages of appreciation. These languages were uncovered by Gary Chapman while helping couples forge stronger relationships, but they've crept into the broader field of personal development because the capacity to provide effective appreciation is a hallmark of Thriving Leadership.

THE FIVE LANGUAGES OF APPRECIATION:

WORDS
This one is obvious and easy. Use words of encouragement and kindness to directly thank or acknowledge people. But it's more than just saying "thank you." Make your gratitude

personal by identifying the specific behaviour or trait that you appreciate. Take appreciation to another level in the way you incorporate it into regular conversation. For example, the language used when you need something can be framed in an appreciative manner. Instead of "demanding" language, such as "This is top priority, I need it by Friday," use "requesting" language, such as "Remember last month when we had that tight deadline on the make-or-break project? And you came through for us? Well, we have another deadline and I'm wondering if you are up the challenge we've got in front of us? We need to have it out by Friday."

ACTS OF SERVICE

Perform deeds that help people or advance ideas within their sphere of interest. Go out of your way to help them move a project forward, participate in a cause that is important to them, or take time to send them a hand-written note. Smile in their presence. Remember the two critical times in every encounter with someone: when you meet and when you depart. Whether it is someone you see every day or only once a year, use these critical moments to convey the message that you appreciate them.

GIFTS

Gifts are tangible. They may be purchased, but gifts don't have to cost money. Gifts may be found (in a closet or file, in a magazine clipping) or made (by you or someone else). The most important aspect is that the gift must be meaningful to the other person, personally or professionally. Often the greatest gift you can give to someone is the gift of your time and undivided attention.

QUALITY TIME

Engage in activities they enjoy (recreation, volunteer, civic, social, whatever). Since it may not be something you particularly enjoy, your focus needs to be on why you are doing it and not on what you are doing. When in conversation, ensure it is distraction-free, make eye contact, smile, listen for feelings, don't interrupt, ask questions and notice body language. Discuss topics of interest to them.

TOUCH
When it comes to touch, we see how appreciation truly is personal. There is nothing wrong with touch in the workplace as long as it is appropriate touch. It might be a handshake, a neck rub, high-five, fist-bump, or a pat on the shoulder, and for some it might be a hug. Be sensitive to the relationship you have and the social setting you are within.

"Appreciation is a wonderful thing: It makes what is excellent in others belong to us as well." —Voltaire

Regardless of the language, be creative, and remember, you must be genuine with your gratitude. Do it with no expectation of reciprocation. Equally important is knowing that every person has a primary language (and a secondary preference for another of the languages). While there is some overlap between the five languages, when you express your gratitude, appreciation is more effectively received when it's spoken in the recipient's primary language. So be mindful to say thank you in their primary language. The ongoing challenge with appreciation is that when you express it, you tend to default to your primary language of appreciation because that's what you know and love best.

Become a master at identifying people's primary language of appreciation. Here are some tips to help you sort out people's languages, including your own. And while nothing is 100% certain, you will home in on their language with a little bit of effort. Gary Chapman has written extensively on the five languages and his books are well worth reading to learn more. In the meantime, ask these questions for insights into someone's primary language:

- In which of the languages do I/they normally express appreciation?
- In which of the languages do I/they ask for appreciation?
- What drives me/them crazy about what others do? Often this is the opposite of your/their primary language. For example:
  - people who never say thank you—WORDS
  - someone who takes the last cup of coffee and doesn't make a fresh pot—ACTS OF SERVICE
  - not receiving something on a special occasion—GIFTS
  - someone who avoids being in proximity to another—TOUCH
  - people who do all the talking and never listen to what you have to say—QUALITY TIME.

Figure out your own language first, and then that of the people closest to you, and be conscious of using their language when you say thank you.

One of the best examples of this is my personal experience with my wife, Lyn. My primary language is words, so for years, on our anniversary, I would express my appreciation and love to her in words. It might have gone something like this, "Happy Anniversary, Hon. Hard to believe we've been together 10 years. We've been through a lot. We've had some huge challenges but we made it through them all. But as I look back, it's been a joy to be together and I appreciate all the support and love you give to our marriage."

Year after year, the words would change some and each

time I thought I hit a home run out of the park. But no. Lyn didn't feel fully appreciated. When I learned about the five languages, I discovered her language was gifts, which helped me understand why she put so much importance on giving a greeting card. So the next year, I got her a greeting card— the humourous variety, because that's what we gave to each other in my family, other than Mom, who always gave "goosh cards," as we called them. It turns out the words on the card are important too, at least to the most important person in my life.

So today, I no longer get hung up on the fact that the poetic phrases inscribed on the card were written by somebody else, that the card is printed in bulk by the thousands, and that the card costs half as much as this book. If I truly want to express my appreciation to my wife and have her hear me, none of these facts matter. All that matters is what matters to her. So that's what I aim for now.

THE HABITS ARE INTERCONNECTED

I'm happy to report that the habits are interconnected, which should be exciting for anyone interested in leadership. Here's why: When you use and practice these habits, you impact, influence and inspire others to positive action, which is what Thriving Leadership is all about. Habits 1 and 2 are for you. As I've already stressed, you need them to feed and fuel yourself as a leader. Habits 3 and 4 are the visible habits that others will see and gain inspiration from. When you practice habits 3 and 4 (sharing what you're grateful for and saying thank you), your actions contribute more positivity to the world around you. Your example will positively influence others and help them reframe their life circumstances (regardless of where they are in the surviving to thriving hierarchy) so that they, too, can spend more time thriving and less time surviving.

MAKING THE HABITS STICK

There is a common misconception that it takes 21 days to make something a habit. In reality, the time it takes for a habit to become automatic depends on a number of factors, such as the complexity of the task, which means a habit can take somewhere between 18 and 254 days before it is automatic.

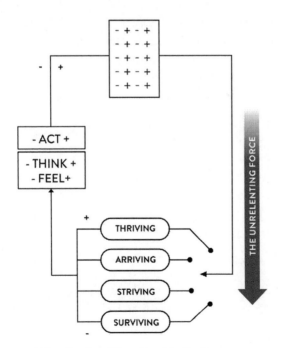

The Cycle of Leadership Influence

Through building these habits you are developing and strengthening your gratitude muscles. Remember, neuroplasticity allows us to reshape our brains via repeated practise. In terms of the Cycle of Leadership Influence, you are helping ensure that the filter your brain uses to make sense of the world is the Thriving Mindset.

Think for a moment about a habit that I suspect is already automatic: brushing your teeth. I'm guessing that you brushed your teeth this morning. Further I'm willing to bet your toothbrush and toothpaste could be found next to the sink or in the vanity. This makes it easy for you to keep the habit of brushing your teeth. I would have been very surprised to hear that you keep your toothbrush in the attic and the toothpaste in the garage. When I've asked dentists what habit is the best predictor of optimal oral health, the only answer I've heard so far is "brushing your teeth." Yes, you should floss and visit the dentist, but daily brushing is the best predictor. Most of us have organized our lives in such a way so that we don't have to think about what we need to do for optimal oral health.

Given that a grateful frame of mind is the best predictor of living a thriving life and being a Thriving Leader, does it make sense that we do a few things to organize our lives in such a way so that we don't have to think about what we need to do to live a thriving life? Go back and reread the 4 habits and the tips for each.

The next chapter brings it all together and connects the thriving grateful mindset to living a meaningful, purpose-led life. While this may seem elusive, it is within anyone's reach. If I was able to find it, I know you can, too.

NINTH LAW OF GRATEFUL LEADERSHIP

HABITS CAN BE LEARNED

IMPLICATIONS FOR YOU:
Develop the four habits for yourself, and spend more time thriving. Set yourself up for success by making the habits as easy as possible to implement so that they will become automatic and habitual.

Don't worry about making anyone else more grateful. For now, focus on yourself, and never ease up on developing and growing as a person. This is not selfish, as you'll be helping others to be more grateful through your leadership example.

Don't let your guard down. Hold on to and remind yourself of the belief, "I am worthy and have lots to be grateful for."

ASK YOURSELF THE FOLLOWING QUESTIONS:

How will I record my gratitudes? Where and when will I do this in my day?

How will I get inspiration from other people by reading or listening to their gratitudes?

With whom will I share my gratitudes each day? Will this look different for the various areas of my life?

What daily occurrence can I use as my reminder to "say thank you"?

KNOWING WHAT I KNOW, WHAT DO I TAKE AWAY FROM THIS CHAPTER?

CHAPTER 10

LIVE A GRATEFUL, PURPOSE-LED LIFE

ONE OF THE DEEPEST desires in my life is to know I've made a difference.

The story I described in Chapter 2 about getting started on coaching is so important, it bears repeating. I give a lot of credit to finding my purpose to Robbie, my boss in the early 2000's. He was the one who suggested I work with an executive coach. Robbie took his leadership role very seriously. He had a knack of balancing his high standards for results with his genuine care for people, and he was committed to my growth and development. If you recall, it was after that initial coaching session, Keith said, "Steve, I'm here for you 24/7. We have our regularly scheduled times to speak, but if for any reason you need me, just call. I'm here."

And then came the day I took him up on his offer and arrived at his studio in tears, feeling like I was drifting without purpose.

Keith immediately put me at ease with his gentle smile, the warm greeting of his hug and the sound of water falling down the sides of the fountain wall in his studio. "So how can I help, Steve?"

I explained that I felt meaning and purpose in my family, because I didn't want him to think that I didn't appreciate my beautiful children and wife. I believe my purpose in my family is related to but different than my purpose based on my unique skills and abilities.

Then I said, "In some ways it feels like I'm living two lives, my professional life and my personal life, and they're not connected. I know I have a purpose, Keith, but it doesn't feel like that."

Keith looked at me and said, "At least you know, Steve. At least you know. Do you know how many people out there don't know they have a purpose? Take heart in the fact that you know you have a purpose and have patience, because your purpose will become clear to you."

When I heard his words, it was as if the weight of the world had been lifted from my shoulders. Somehow he gave me solace and I was excited by the anticipation I could feel, because I believed Keith. Fortunately, that sense of peace stuck, because it took another two or three years before my purpose would start to become clear.

My purpose came into focus as my ah-ha moment, which was realizing "it was as if my life was handed to me on a silver platter," converged with the end of classes in my graduate program. Not only did my purpose become clear, but the next step became clear, which led to my initial research study on gratitude.

Today, I express my purpose in terms of my dream: One billion happier people. And it is this purpose that keeps me teaching gratitude, because I now know that gratitude is the key to a happier, thriving life.

My purpose is the reason I was put on this planet in terms of my unique skills and abilities. At present, I'm not sure how my dream will come true, so I take comfort in the common ground I share with the likes of Gandhi, Kennedy and King (and that's probably all I have in common with these great leaders), who didn't know how their dream would come true. I've also had to come to grips with how my purpose integrated with my personal life, because my family is the most important part of my life. Which is more important, my life purpose or my family? I've come to realize that I was asking the wrong question. For example, in my family I take on different roles, and each of these roles is a gift, for which I'm grateful. I'm a son, brother, husband, father and grandfather and in each of these roles I feel called to treasure that gift in alignment with my life purpose. While my view on this may change at some point in the future, my family constitutes the most important (to me) of the one billion people. And in my family, my wife Lyn is the most important person in the world.

This is a bit of an aside, but important. The struggle in finding my purpose itself has been a great gift to me. It has led to countless coffee conversations with colleagues and friends who found themselves in career transition or wondering what was next. I made the simple decision to be there for anyone who wanted to talk about their next chapter. I can't tell you how many of these conversations I've had, but these chats trigger emotions across the spectrum: tears, laughter, anger, excitement, fear and hope. They are always inspiring and uplifting.

THE POWER OF PURPOSE

Purpose is powerful. This idea has been at the center of personal development since its inception. James Allen talked about purpose more than 100 years ago in *As a Man Thinketh* as did Napoleon Hill in *Think and Grow Rich*. In recent years the whole idea of purpose and knowing your "why" has gained increasing attention through many authors and speakers.

Here is a story about hockey that illustrates the power or purpose. The playoffs and lead-up to the Stanley Cup finals are a grueling two and a half months for the players and teams. The travel is constant and there's a game almost every second day on top of practice and working out. The games are tougher and players spend a lot of time away from their families, even when games are in their home city. While I've never been in the dressing room of a championship team, I asked Joe, who has won the Stanley Cup, "Did you guys complain about how hard it was? Did you guys slack off because you didn't think it was fair you had to spend so much time away from your family? Did you hear people complain because you were tired and needed more rest?"

To every question, he said, "No. There was never any complaining. Everyone showed up and gave their best."

Why do you think that is? It's because these players knew exactly why they were doing what they were doing. They had a purpose and it was crystal clear. You show me a team or an individual that fights and bickers and I'll show you a team or a person who's lost their purpose.

WHAT IS YOUR PURPOSE?

Keith's words still ring in my ears, "At least you know you have a purpose." At the time I asked him, "You mean there are people out there who don't know they have a purpose?"

"Yes, Steve." he said.

Talk about getting blindsided by one's worldview. I was

so hung up on finding my purpose, I assumed everyone just knew they had a purpose. Seligman recognizes purpose in his model for human flourishing, as PERMA includes "meaning" and "achievement" as two of the pillars in the model. As humans, we long to make a difference in the world. So for you, what is your deepest desire when you think about the ultimate difference you want to make in the world? Is your dream for your family, for the kids you raise, for the community that supported you? How are you using the gifts and talents with which you've been blessed? You have a purpose.

It doesn't matter what your purpose is. It only matters that you discover it. If your purpose is not clear to you, that's OK. Look to your past, look at your gifts and talents and make a list of what you're grateful for. After all, these are gifts, so they are something to be grateful for. Then find a way to use your gifts in service to the world, which is Habit 4 (Say thank you). The way I see it, living out your purpose is an expression of gratitude, a way of saying thank you for the gifts you've received.

It is our individual responsibility to find and hone our purpose. There are many books and mentors who can teach you about defining your purpose. I don't know if the purpose experts would classify my purpose (one billion happier people) as the proper way to define one's purpose or not. For now, my purpose is inspiring for me, so my only advice is to define your purpose in a way that is meaningful and inspiring to you.

It is very rewarding to know and live with a purpose. If your purpose is unclear, be patient and be kind to yourself, because if you're like me, I struggled to find my purpose, so it may take some time before it becomes clear to you.

SOLVING WORLD PROBLEMS

When I went to high school, there was a popular (which is code for easy) course called Modern World Problems. I did not take the course, but if it was offered today, what topics do you think would be studied and discussed? It would probably include issues like globalization, global warming, discrimination and privilege, water, and sustainability. In spite of these huge challenges, we live in a time where people have never been freer, more educated, more connected, and wealthier. Yet, in the western world, according to the 2018 World Happiness Report, happiness has remained virtually unchanged for the past 50 years.

In the workplace, Gallup continues to report that 70% of the global workforce is not engaged in their work. This 70% statistic has hardly budged since Gallup began measuring it. Decades have passed and billions of dollars have been poured into making the workplace a spot where people can thrive and based on what Gallup reports, all this time and investment is a complete failure. Given that we spend almost half of our waking hours at work and there's such a low level of emotional commitment to work, it's more than a complete failure; it's a tragedy.

I don't believe that we are destined to this 70% statistic, but clearly we have to do something different.

As a society, we have advanced so much, but we're no happier. How can this be? As a species we have laboured to build societies in which every single person can thrive, and it is failing because far too many people remain stuck struggling, never having enough.

I suspect this dilemma is the work of the unrelenting force, because we've adapted to all of the marvelous progress, which leaves us thinking and feeling we need more. Think about it: we get upset if the internet is slow and it takes a few extra seconds to download our email while we're at 35,000 feet flying across the country. We know gratitude is the antidote to first world problems and to being stuck in survival mode. Whether gratitude and gratitude alone will solve global happiness, I can't be 100% certain, but the growing body of research is telling us that gratitude transforms surviving into thriving and that gratitude is the key to happiness.

I believe gratitude has the potential to solve some of the world's largest problems. Happier people means fewer wars. Happier people means less poverty. Happier people means less violence. Happier people means more freedom. Happier people means more generosity. Ultimately, happier people means a better world for you and those you care for.

Solving world problems might sound grandiose, but even the smallest of interactions makes a difference. Even seemingly insignificant actions matter. This has been proven every single day in my life. Whenever I am at a cash register or service center—a grocery store, coffee shop, gas station, at reception in an office, on the phone with someone at a contact center, I make a point to ask, "How is your day going?" I don't ask it right away. After we both get "Hi, how are you?" out of the way, then I make eye contact, ask my question and I stop to listen. People always take a few moments to share a little bit about their day. Most of the time, they respond positively; occasionally I'll get a negative response, and a few times I've even had people share intensely challenging personal situations that brought them to tears. It's easy to discount the impact something like this has, but it always results in a positive experience for both of us. It's a very simple but meaningful way to connect with another human being, a complete stranger, who is helping me. I believe it makes a difference and contributes to the type of world I want to live in.

That simple question is one of the ways I practice Habit 4 and say thank you.

CAUTION: MONEY

Money is a valued possession in society. Money is so treasured and sought after that it can sometimes be confusing as to whether we possess our money or our money possesses us. All this attention and desire for more money is a concerning source of stress and anxiety, the breeding ground for disease.

Years ago, I was at church and anxiously listening to the pastor who was talking about money. The more he spoke, the more I resisted his message by thinking, "This is my money. Who are you to tell me what to do with my money?" I really can't recall the point he was trying to make because all I heard was someone who was threatening me and my money. I was in survival mode because I felt threatened. Today I realize that what got me upset had nothing to do with what the pastor said. Instead it had everything to do with my relationship with what I considered "my money." I felt I was entitled to my money because I had earned it. It was all me, therefore it was all mine. I was attached to my money, so much so that it controlled me.

Money and the accumulation of wealth have little to do with leading a purposeful life.

When it comes to money, thriving does not mean being a multi-millionaire. There is a base level of wealth that is connected to happiness. We know happiness increases as income rises, but happiness from money plateaus around $75,000 year. Beyond that, there is little connection between happiness and wealth, neither absolute wealth (i.e. someone's net worth is $1M) nor relative wealth (i.e. someone's net worth is more than their neighbour's net worth). In either case, if we are not grateful for the level of wealth that we have, we will succumb to the unrelenting force by adapting to our level of wealth and end up thinking and feeling that we need more. And this will never change.

We are back in survival mindset when we think we don't have enough money. We thrive when we realize we have enough money. We must focus on the money we have, not on what we don't have. The secret to being grateful for money is to see it as a gift. When we see the wealth we have and the income we earn as a gift (yes even in spite of the fact that we worked hard for it), we are on the road to thriving with money. If you are like I was, thinking I was the self-made man, it may take some effort to see money as a gift. But as I began to see the support I had from my parents growing up and through school, I realized I couldn't have done it on my own. When I think of the people who supported me in my part-time jobs and served as references to help me secure a full time job as an engineer, I realized it wasn't all me. When I think of my professors and teachers who helped me learn and understand what I needed to earn a good income, I realized it wasn't all me. In the end I came to the conclusion that yes, I had to put in the effort and work. But I had been given so much by so many people that, in fact, the opportunity to be an engineer was truly a gift for which I was immensely grateful.

But how can someone thrive when their income is less than $75,000? And what about people who live on less than $20,000 per year? While it is more difficult at $20,000, if we want to thrive, we need to focus on what we have, and not focus on what we don't have. Thriving enables us to see the good and not be consumed by the bad, putting us in a much better frame of mind to do something about our situations. We must take the time to develop the Four Habits and deliberately look for the good in our lives. If e look for good, e will find it. It may start small with things, like food in the fridge, power that has not been disconnected for a month, or a job where we are not harassed. We start here and expand. There will be no end to the challenges of life, be they financial, health-related, relationships. In spite of the challenges, we must not let down our guard. If we hold tightly to the belief that we are worthy and have much to be grateful for, we create the conditions to more easily find the good so we're better equipped to deal with the crap. I don't believe it will serve anyone well if we create a list of exceptions, be it lack of money, poor health, or toxic relationships, to justify a surviving mindset.

Having more money isn't the simple answer to spending more time thriving, either. For example, if we have a higher socio-economic standing, we are by definition less reliant on others. Research has found this makes us less likely to be empathetic and less grateful, based on taking credit for our own success.

MY PURPOSE APPEARED
ALMOST OUT OF THIN AIR

It was late November 2003, a day or two before my final class in my graduate program. We had one final assignment which required us to update and submit our values and our purpose statement. My work with Keith on values and purpose had helped me a great deal on this, but I was still drawing a blank on my purpose.

The next morning I walked into my office and someone had left a job posting on my desk encouraging me to apply. It was for the CEO position at one of our region's largest and most respected charities. While it was nice to think someone thought I could take on this role, it was their note that really hit home. It said, "This has you written all over it."

To remind you of the context at this point in my life, I had experienced my ah-ha moment in realizing my life was a gift. I had the accompanying sense of overwhelming gratitude, and I was aware of my need to say thank you, although I didn't call it Habit 4 at the time.

And as I looked at the note, it struck me. The job is about helping people express their inborn need to say thank you. And the light went on for me. I had found my purpose. The wording is different today than in my initial business plan but it remains rooted in gratitude. At the time, I expressed it this way:

I am the catalyst that ignites the latent passion of giving in people.

This formed the basis for my graduate research on gratitude, where we found that gratitude was at the core of generosity. Ultimately, in 2006, I convinced my wife of 21 years that I should quit my job and start a business to make this dream a reality. Lyn was and continues to be a huge supporter for me. I began down the path to realize my purpose by expanding gratitude, which ultimately led me to begin hosting conversations and teaching the very basics of gratefulness.

Today, my purpose is expressed as my dream:

One billion happier people.

It is still rooted in gratitude. Basically, I'm a teacher, and I teach one of the simplest lessons out there: be grateful, and you'll be happy, so you can live a thriving life. This provides a great sense of purpose and reinforces every day that what we do makes a difference.

It's interesting to see how the expression of my purpose has evolved over the years. It is no longer focused on me. Instead it is focused on others and what I desire for a better world.

I had thought that making a difference was reserved for those with grand ideas or blessed with multi-million dollar fortunes. I've come to learn from the unrelenting hugs from our daughter Stephanie at age five, the smiles on people I pass on the sidewalk, and the thank yous I've received, that our actions matter. Every action matters.

Coming full circle, the First Law of Grateful Leadership, "no one is self-made," provides an infinite source of inspiration for experiencing gratitude and acknowledges the innate value in the unique person you are. It provides the inspiration for you to express your gratitude. And we know that when you express your gratitude, it matters.

My challenge to you is to be the thriving leader you're meant to be, and to inspire positive action in those around you.

TENTH LAW OF GRATEFUL LEADERSHIP

YOU MAKE A DIFFERENCE

IMPLICATIONS FOR YOU

Through your actions, no matter how large or small, you make a difference and you are important, because you are uniquely you. No one else is you and no matter how broken or perfect you feel, you are important. Believe it.

Do not doubt your contributions. Ruminate over the idea that you make a difference. And in spite of the self doubt which will creep into your mind, I encourage you to act, to do something, in essence, to say thank you.

ASK YOURSELF THE FOLLOWING QUESTIONS:

What is my purpose and dream for the world?

As I look at my life, how has the lack of money, or abundance of money, impacted my happiness?

How might I more quickly overcome self doubt when it sets in (which it will inevitably)?

How will I ensure gratitude remains an active ongoing part of my life?

KNOWING WHAT I KNOW, WHAT DO I TAKE AWAY FROM THIS CHAPTER?

WHAT'S NEXT?

CONGRATULATIONS! THANKS FOR INVESTING your life into reading this book. My hope is that you've gained a few gratitude tools to help you spend more time thriving and less time merely surviving.

Over the coming weeks and months, I encourage you to practice and master the four gratitude habits:

- Make a list of what you're grateful for
- Read or listen to what others are grateful for
- Share your gratitudes with others
- Say thank you

Take advantage of resources available to you to help make these habits automatic. You can work these habits into your daily routine, and it should take no more than four to eight minutes to incorporate all four into your day. Remind yourself that gratitude is not something we're using to fix people who are broken. It's not because anyone is broken, rather it's about helping people grow so that they can develop a mindset that spends more time thriving and less time surviving.

Clarify your purpose and make it your way of expressing your gratitude to the world. It's your way of uniquely saying thank you for all you've received.

While I want you to introduce gratitude to as many people as possible, please do so in the spirit of wanting people to spend more time thriving versus needing to correct a behaviour. Set the example of Thriving Leadership in all you do. Share your gratitudes with them. Ask them questions like, "What's the best part of your day so far?" Share your experience of growth on your gratitude journey and what having a more grateful mindset has done for you. All the while, remain non-judgmental and supportive.

For example, as kids we would complain about the supper meal. I'm sure Mom and Dad probably wanted to tell us we should be grateful to have food on the table. But they didn't, because they knew that it wouldn't work if they tried to force us to be grateful. They knew we had to find that gratitude ourselves.

When you are a thriving leader and possess a thriving mindset, people will notice it in you, and your gratitude will spread to them naturally. It's infectious.

Lastly, you matter and what you do makes a difference. Thank you.

MY FINAL GRATITUDE LIST

Writing a book was a big accomplishment for me and I am grateful to many many people for being a part of this accomplishment.

I'm grateful for my book team at Happful.com:

- Calvin Simpson who quarterbacked the effort and always appeared with a thriving mindset.
- Alaina Leary who delicately and passionately encouraged and challenged me throughout the writing process. I loved our weekly calls.
- Xavier Comas for so quickly digesting the foundational ideas and transforming them into a simple yet powerful visual.
- Victoria Barrett for your eye and attention to detail from so many perspectives. Your editing made the book gooder.

I'm grateful for my friends, professional colleagues and writing encouragers:

- Al MacKinnon and Derek Flynn for being best friends with whom I can talk about anything—we've come a long way since we met in Grade 6.

- Peter Chapman for our regular coffee meetings at our usual location where many ideas were born.
- Linda Wilson for your trust and commitment to gratitude and growth.
- Nancy MacKay for your inspiration and your fervent support.
- The Daily Gratitudes Community who inspire me with your gratitudes each weekday.

I'm grateful for my family:
- Mom who instilled in us that we have lots to be grateful for and for the positivity that you oozed.
- Dad who has deep relationships with all your descendants and your support for us all. Your perspective is always insightful.
- My brothers Pete, Mike and Greg and my sister Jan with whom we share a special bond that is hard to describe in words.
- Our kids, Nick and Stef and grandson Max, who are our pride and joy. You bring such light into my life by being who you are.
- FD and Mae for raising a wonderful daughter and for being a gracious second set of parents to me.
- My Queen, Lyn for your unending support and all you put up with. You complete me and you epitomize caring.

I'm grateful for all the people whose first names are included in the stories of this book and for the clients I've had the privilege to serve over the past 12 years. You shaped my journey so you are a part of who I am. You are truly dear to me.

And I'm grateful to the countless others who contributed to my freedom, education, healthcare, safety, food, entertainment, recreation and more.

Made in the USA
San Bernardino, CA
16 June 2019